"Mark Riddle's Inside the Mind of Youth Pastors speaks boldly, intelligently, and practically to the critical issues and crises of local church youth ministry. Mark exhibits exceptional skill in going beneath the superficial assumptions to engage the heart and soul of the complex dance between senior pastors, parents, and youth pastors. This book corrects common mistakes and provokes creative thought about vibrant, enduring youth ministry. I'm honored to call Mark Riddle a good friend."

—Dr. John W. Frye, pastor, Fellowship Evangelical Covenant Church, Hudsonville, Michigan

"Inside the Mind of Youth Pastors a combination of engaged thought, discernment, and experience from a seasoned youth ministry veteran. Mark Riddle engages us with the tough questions underlying our motives in youth ministry and prompts us to change for the better. A serious reading of this book will help congregations of all sizes and denominations overcome the constant cycle of hiring and losing youth pastors, pastors understand how to mentor and work cohesively with their youth pastors, and youth pastors develop a solid ideology for the orientation of their ministries."

—Dan Mayes, pastor, First Christian Church of Spencer, Iowa

"Inside the Mind of Youth Pastors unlocks how to move from a youth pastor-centered ministry to one the whole church—even the senior pastor—believes in and participates in. Forthright yet disarmingly fun to read and talk about for non-anxious leaders ready to rethink the hiring process with a longer view. Riddle has drawn from years of consulting nationwide in youth ministry and packed this book with a truckload of wisdom. Church leaders wanting to staff and lead healthy, sustainable youth ministries will do well to remember the three Rs: Riddle...Really...Rocks."

—Greg Taylor, associate minister, Garnett Church of Christ; senior editor, Wineskins.org

"Over the last three decades, youth ministry has rapidly matured as a profession, and the literature has struggled to keep pace. One of the gaping holes has been a thoughtful, practical handbook to help other church staff members, youth-education committees, parents, and others really understand what youth ministry is all about. Until now. Through Inside the Mind of Youth Pastors, Mark Riddle has given the church a gift. Filled with wisdom from his years as a youth pastor and youth ministry consultant, rife with real-life stories, and peppered with excellent discussion questions, this book promises to build a bridge from the often lonely island of youth ministry back to the rest of the church staff and the many others in churches who care about youth ministry but often struggle to understand it. Every church staff in America should work through this book."

—Tony Jones, author, *Postmodern Youth Ministry: Exploring Cultural Shift, Cultivating Authentic Community, and Creating Holistic Connections* and *The New Christians: Dispatches from the Emergent Frontier*

"Churches can so easily screw up talented youth pastors! Leaders need to hire the right people and learn to manage them effectively to allow youth pastors and their ministries to thrive. Mark Riddle knows youth ministry inside and out and has so much wisdom and good advice to offer. I wholeheartedly endorse this book."

—**Mark Russell, CEO, Church Army UK and Ireland (youth pastor in Ireland and London, 1997-2006)**

"It's been said that pain and frustration is the gap between expectation and reality. Mark Riddle provides the practical tools necessary to navigate the oft-overlooked distance between a youth pastor and senior pastor. All senior pastors looking to create an open dialogue and healthy understanding of their student ministry pastors would benefit from the compelling ideas presented in this book."

—**Steve Carter, kids + students pastor, Mars Hill Church**

"Most churches go through a youth pastor every couple of years. Why are so many mistakes made both hiring and developing youth pastors? I'll tell you why...people didn't read and heed Mark Riddle's wisdom-packed book, Inside the Mind of Youth Pastors. Do your church, students, and future youth pastor a favor and read this book before you hire the next one."

—Dan Webster, founder, Authentic Leadership, Inc.

"Mark Riddle has offered a great tool for those looking to start or improve a relationship with a youth pastor. The issues he addresses are vital to a healthy ministry environment on both sides of the coin. Well illustrated with the safe 'someone I know' stories, Inside the Mind of Youth Pastors will ease tension and get to the heart of the matter in the most challenging situations involving the search, hiring, and support of those who work with students in churches. The questions for discussion included in each chapter will benefit any church-staff relationship, and Mark's insight and tested advice gives a feeling of hope. Well done Mark!"

—Rev. Scott Kail, pastor to students, Piedmont (California) Community Church

"Mark Riddle succinctly—and sometimes with playful illustrations about 35-pound raccoons—points the way to connecting youth with God in Inside the Mind of Youth Pastors. Rather than outsourcing ministry, Mark describes and walks us through an evaluative look at ministry via relationships. His conversation with us goes beyond the polarities of purpose-driven versus program-driven; it instead considers a relationship-centered youth ministry. Join Mark on his 'deck' for this conversation about relationships and roles, systems and structures, and the means to connect youth with the Kingdom of God and adults who love them."

—Todd Littleton, pastor, Snow Hill Baptist Church, Tuttle, Oklahoma; consultant with the Riddle Group; executive director of ETREK Collaborative Learning Journeys; education consultant with Shapevine.com

"I applaud all pastors who read and discuss this book with their youth pastors. I couldn't help but chuckle as I read these pages. If only my first pastor had read this book...things might have gone differently!"

—Brandon Grissom, worship leader and creative director, Axis, Willow Creek Community Church, South Barrington, Illinois

"I've had the privilege of watching Mark Riddle put what's written in this book into practice. He's done a tremendous job helping our church get a better sense of how and why we do what we do in our student ministry. Mark writes from experience—and not just his own, but also the experience of countless other church leaders and youth pastors he's counseled, mentored, and challenged. As a senior leader in my church, some of what Mark writes makes me uncomfortable. He keeps reminding me that the church isn't a machine, and the members of my staff aren't moving parts that can be easily replaced. Instead they're human beings created in the image of God who deserve equal parts compassion and truth if they're to grow to their full potential. My favorite chapter is where Mark unpacks the "Ladder of Inference." It was great to finally understand why people misunderstand some of what I say and do. Then I realized I'm guilty of climbing the ladder just as quickly as anybody else. Thanks Mark."

—Wade Hodges, lead minister, Garnett Church of Christ, Tulsa, Oklahoma

"Intentionality...that's what most of our churches are missing as we think about and do youth ministry. Sadly, it usually starts from the moment we establish a youth ministry and then look for a 'professional' to "fill the spot.' In many cases, it winds up being a recipe for disaster or mediocrity as best. Mark Riddle issues a challenge and a how-to regarding our need to stop, think, and plan. Pastors, search committees, and youth workers will find Mark's suggestions and guidance to be thought-provoking and helpful so you can act wisely now."

—Walt Mueller, president, Center for Parent/Youth Understanding; author, *Youth Culture 101*

"If a church is searching for a youth pastor, the first step it needs to take is to buy this book for every member of the search committee. Mark saves churches (and youth workers) countless hours and countless dollars by asking critical questions that need to be answered before anyone signs on the dotted line."

—**Ginny Olson, Center for Youth Ministry Studies,**
North Park University & North Park Seminary

"It's a fact. The health of a church staff directly impacts the health of a church. It's also true that hiring a youth minister for the wrong reasons can decimate a church. Mark Riddle understands this from his years of serving on a staff and his consulting with hundreds of churches. In fact, reading this book is like having Mark personally consult with your church—at a much-reduced price! He's straightforward, yet gracious, asking the questions all churches need to grapple with before they hire their next youth pastors. Inside the Mind of Youth Pastors is filled with countless real-life examples of both healthy and unhealthy churches that will help readers discover where their churches reside. Perhaps most importantly, Mark's passion for helping churches develop healthy staff—and subsequently healthy ministries—literally drips from the pages as he provides solid and substantial help for churches of all sizes and traditions. As someone who's studied for more than two decades the relationship between hiring a youth minister and the success of the youth ministry, I heartily endorse this book as one that all who're involved in the search for a youth pastor should read."

—**James K. Hampton, author, speaker, veteran youth worker,**
and associate professor of youth ministry at Asbury Theological
Seminary

"Mark helps us navigate through the minefields of youth ministry. If you're looking for something healthy and sustainable, you've found it."

—**Dan Kimball, author, *They Like Jesus but Not the Church***

"No more games. No more e-Harmony-esque youth pastor searches. No more faith communities trying to act like businesses or military operations. Let's make church beautiful and let's see if youth ministry can guide the way. Riddle's book contributes to this vision. This book will terrify you. It'll ask you to be honest about who you are and what you want. Don't even think about hiring someone or taking a youth pastor job until you read this book. I'm increasingly convinced that the more we look for what we want in others, the more clearly we see ourselves. Before churches post that youth pastor job description, or individuals send that resume, read this book. Riddle takes you on an important journey. His short chapters demand long, thoughtful answers. So here's my warning: The self-perception churches or individuals hold as they begin reading this book may be very different by the time they get to the end of it."

—Steve Argue, adjunct professor of youth ministry and executive director of the Contextual Learning Center at Grand Rapids Theological Seminary; cofounder, Intersect, Inc.

"I can't get Riddle out of my head! Riddle freakishly resides in the inner-recesses of the minds of all of us who consider ourselves youth pastors. If you're a church leader, you need this book to serve as your field guide—or maybe in some cases, your survival guide. Quick! Snatch it up and journey deep into the head (and ultimately the heart) of your youth pastor and find out what makes that person one of a kind."

—Chris Folmsbee, author, *A New Kind of Youth Ministry*; chief ministries officer (CMO), YouthFront

"Attention Senior Pastors: This book isn't just about youth ministry. It will unlock the secret you've been looking for: How to connect with young families on their terms! Mark Riddle lets you behind the curtain in this guided tour of a relevant youth ministry and its role in the 21st-century family. With a straightforward and step-by-step process, you, too, can grow a youth ministry that introduces young people to the love of Jesus and supports families as they seek their full place in God's kingdom. The chapter on 'Unfunny Jokes the Church Keeps Telling' is worth the price of the whole book."

—Jonathan Reitz, principal, The Leader Shed, Cleveland, Ohio

INSIDE THE MIND
OF YOUTH PASTORS

PREP SMALL GROUP LEADERS

CREATE MESSAGE OUTLINE

HOPES FOR CHURCH

DESIRE FOR MENTOR

MEET WITH JOHN'S PARENTS

A CHURCH LEADER'S GUIDE TO STAFFING AND LEADING YOUTH PASTORS

Mark Riddle

ZONDERVAN®

ZONDERVAN.com/
AUTHORTRACKER
follow your favorite authors

youth
specialties

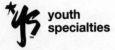

Inside the Mind of Youth Pastors: A Church Leader's Guide to Staffing and Leading Youth Pastors
Copyright 2009 by Mark Riddle

Youth Specialties resources, 300 S. Pierce St., El Cajon, CA 92020 are published by Zondervan, 5300 Patterson Ave. SE, Grand Rapids, MI 49530.

ISBN 978-0-310-28365-2

Cover design by Toolbox Studios
Interior design by Mark Novelli, IMAGO MEDIA

Printed in the United States of America

09 10 11 12 13 14 • 20 19 18 17 16 15 14 13 12 11 10 9 8 7 6 5 4 3 2 1

AUTHOR'S NOTE

This book is filled with information gathered from research, interviews, and observation. Every story in this book is true, though there are a few instances in which I chose to merge several stories into one. Moreover, these stories are not unique to individual churches or pastors. In fact, you may find yourself relating to many of the people and circumstances recounted in this book. This makes each story *everyone's* story. So, if you recognize yourself in a story, chances are it's about you—you and many others.

I'd also like you to consider this book the beginning of a conversation between the two of us. While it contains many of the concepts and principles I've learned from my research, there are several ideas that did not fit within the scope of this writing—and others that are still being formed. Continued conversation with you will afford us the opportunity to keep learning from each other. As you lead your church, I would enjoy hearing about how your story unfolds.

Mark Riddle

Tulsa, Oklahoma

markriddle.net

mark@theRiddleGroup.com

CONTENT

SPECIAL ACKNOWLEDGMENTS

Thanks to Pam, my favorite person in the whole world, for holding down the fort so I could disappear and write.

Thanks to Zachery, Jaden, and Mikayla for keeping me on my toes and being wonderful reminders of what love, beauty, and energy look like.

Thanks to Jeff Dunn for encouraging me to write this book after hearing the title.

Thanks to the great Jay Howver for asking me for the proposal and the great folks at YS and Zondervan for believing I had something to say.

Thanks to my man, John Raymond.

Thanks to Something in Michigan. Each of you redeemed my hope in the church at a time in my life when I needed it.

Thanks to the Tulsa cohort. You know who you are.

Thanks to Paul Cunningham, Rob Merola, Scott French, Wade Hodges, Jay Henderson, Steve Argue, Jimmy Doyle, David Welch, Mark Oestreicher, Chris Folmsbee, Mike King, Ginny Olson, Jim Hampton, Dan McIntosh, Joe Myers, Todd Littleton, and Jonathon Reitz.

Thanks to Randy Southern for bringing clarity to my thoughts and encouragement to my content.

A special thanks to all the churches who let me drop in every once in a while.

IMPORTANT! A NOTE ABOUT GIFTING THIS BOOK

This book is designed to expand and deepen your relationship with your youth pastor. Being given this book is an overture of camaraderie and reveals a desire to work with you in order to improve the ministry to youth in your church. If your youth pastor gives a copy of this book to you, the senior pastor, please take it as a compliment. Think of this book as the beginning of a new conversation between the two of you—one in which you can learn from each other as leaders.

INTRODUCTION

Healthy. Sustainable. Youth. Ministry.

Ultimately, that's what this book is about: Helping you lead your church toward healthy, sustainable youth ministry. But along the way, guiding a youth pastor can be difficult. Few church leaders receive training on how to manage a staff.

Youth pastors can be difficult to lead for a variety of reasons—the fluidity of their schedules; their strong desire for change, informed by the need to connect the gospel to teenagers; fundamental communication differences. Add to that an anxious congregational or parental climate, and you've got a tricky managerial situation.

I've sat in countless offices over the years as a consultant, listening to senior pastors trying to understand their youth pastors and vice versa. Feeling misunderstood often leads to dysfunction and conflict, so in order to effectively lead a youth pastor, you have to understand her, and she has to understand you. That's where this book comes in. Its purpose is to give you a glimpse inside the mind of a youth pastor. This not only will help you lead your current youth ministry staff, it will also help you understand how to better staff for the position in the future—and better guide your congregation toward a more sustainable youth ministry.

This book is most effective when read by a team. It's designed to facilitate dialogue among your leaders in ministry, and hopefully, within your congregation. It's also designed to help move your ministry toward health.

Of course *health* is a relative term. Some people treat it as a goal or a destination to be reached. When they say, "Our church is healthy," they see it as an achievement, a milestone to be celebrated. And it is—to an extent.

But it's not a finish line. The healthy church that doesn't constantly and purposefully pursue health will become less healthy. Health is a trajectory, not a status. It's the constant, intentional movement toward God's best. A healthy church's status quo is movement. Movement toward the fulfillment of who God created individuals to be. Movement toward a restoration of relationship between God and his people. Movement toward a reconciliation of what it means to love your neighbor and to live within God's creation. This movement toward health is never perfect, but always being perfected. And it requires total dependence on God.

Furthermore, *health* looks different for every church. Various congregations may have very different expressions of health. But one expression that many churches share is the child dedication ceremony—though it may have a different name in your tradition. While you hold a baby in front of the congregation, the parents commit to honoring God where it impacts them the most—their family. They make vows before God and each other. They declare their intention and desire to raise their child in the way of Christ. The words might differ from tradition to tradition, but the meaning is the same. Parents are making a covenant with God in the presence of their church family. What a holy moment! And it gets better.

The congregation plays a part in the ceremony as well. Church members join the parents in a pledge to God, to each other, to the parents, and to the child. As the body of Christ they vow to help raise the child in a God-honoring way. They vow to assist the parents in guiding the child in the way of Christ in the world.

In my experience, few moments in a church's life rival a child dedication or baptism. In a world where young people often feel abandoned by adults, the notion of a community vowing to raise a child is countercultural. Youth ministry (along with children's ministry) is an outgrowth of those vows. It's a vehicle for the congregation to make good on its promises—to the young people of the church and to the young people in the community whose parents are unwilling to make a vow themselves.

That's why a church does youth ministry.

That's why I wrote this book—to help you have the most effective and healthy youth ministry possible. The problem with the book you now hold in your hands is that it's a one-way conversation, which is contrary to the essences of both my personality and great consulting.

I wish instead I could have you over to my house so I could get to know you. We'd sit on the deck in my backyard, and I'd invite you to tell me your story. What do you love? What drives you crazy? What do you read? What team do you root for on Saturday or Sunday afternoons?

I'd love to hear about your church and what makes it tick. I'd love to hear about your youth ministry and your youth pastor, if you have one. I'd love to be a sounding board for you, to answer questions such as, "Is this normal?" or "Should this concern me?" or "Where do I find the right youth pastor for us?" or "How can I let my youth pastor know how much I appreciate her?"

Listening to you is important to me because I believe all ministry is contextual. That's why I wish we could sit down and talk. Maybe one day that will happen. Maybe one day I'll be on your deck. That's my preferred means of communication: Face-to-face—preferably with food. This book is an attempt to answer some of the questions I've answered on my deck and on the decks of church leaders I now call friends.

So please forgive the medium and understand my intent. And maybe we'll enjoy a spring day on a deck together soon.

Section 1

STAFFING FOR YOUTH MINISTRY

Chapter One

WHY DO YOU WANT TO HIRE A YOUTH PASTOR?

I talk to a lot of church leaders every year. Very few are able to articulate why their churches have youth ministries in our first conversation. Every leader has an answer when I ask, but precious few have answers with substance or meaning. The answers range from "We want to make fully devoted followers of Christ" to whatever comes to the leader's mind at that moment.

What are you hoping to accomplish in the lives of teenagers? If your church can't articulate why it has a youth ministry, what are you hiring a youth pastor to do?

Sadly, since most churches can't articulate why they have a youth ministry, the average youth pastor ends up running a bunch of programs that may or may not accomplish what the church is hoping for.

Let's take a look at some of the most popular responses to the question, "Why do you want to hire a youth pastor?"

REASON #1: "WE WANT TO REACH KIDS."

It's encouraging that you and your church are eager to reach teenagers. Chances are, you want to connect with the kids in your church and the kids in the community who have yet to attend your church. It's a solid ambition for a church, but it's *not* an adequate answer to the question, "Why do you want to hire a youth pastor?"

Churches don't need a youth pastor to reach kids. Churches of all shapes and sizes reach kids every week in innovative ways without a paid youth pastor on staff. If your church equates reaching kids with hiring a youth pastor, something's wrong. Don't give up on reaching kids. But let's explore other, healthier reasons to hire a youth pastor.

REASON #2: "WE WANT TO MAKE A DIFFERENCE IN TEENAGERS' LIVES."

To be direct, there aren't enough senior pastors who *really* want to make a difference in teenagers' lives. So this is an exciting response to hear as a consultant. Unfortunately, though, as an answer to our question, it falls way short. There are thousands of people making a difference in the lives of teenagers—and most of them aren't youth pastors. More pointedly, there are plenty of churches making a substantive difference in the lives of teenagers—without a paid youth staff. If your church feels it needs a youth pastor in order to make a difference in the lives of young people, something's wrong.

REASON #3: "I [THE SENIOR PASTOR] DON'T HAVE THE TIME."

The old joke about you working one hour a week—on Sunday morning—isn't funny. The truth is, you have too much on your plate already. There aren't enough hours in the day to add another responsibility—especially something so involved and time consuming as youth ministry. Hiring a youth pastor would immediately take that weight from your shoulders. With so much to do in the church, certainly this is one thing you can hand off to a staff person. Right?

Let's be clear. There's no more difficult job in the church than yours. Your job is more emotionally demanding than most of the people who sit in your congregation will ever know. But hiring a youth pastor for this reason is a very bad idea, one that will hurt you and your church in the long run. (We'll tackle this topic in more detail in chapter 4.)

Don't let today's quick solutions cause tomorrow's long-term problems. Hiring a youth pastor because you're too busy can cause systemic problems that can take your church years to resolve.

REASON #4: "EVERYONE ELSE IS DOING IT."

That seems to be the case, doesn't it? The last 20 years have seen an amazing increase in the population of professional youth ministers. Today it's normal for new church plants to almost immediately hire a youth pastor. While strategically it's probably not the best call for many churches, it is the norm.

If all the other churches were jumping of a cliff, would you? (I'm only sort of joking.) Believe it or not, there are churches that don't have youth pastors, yet are able to minister to youth in tremendous ways. They're able to maintain healthy and growing youth ministries. Conversely, there are churches with full-time staff members who aren't able to connect with young people or their parents. Simply hiring a youth pastor because it's assumed you need one is not a good impetus for staffing.

REASON #5: "PARENTS WANT A YOUTH PASTOR."

The pressure from parents on church leaders to hire a youth pastor is at an all-time high. Today's parents probably had the opportunity to grow up in a youth ministry. Many have meaningful memories of their youth ministry experiences. To them, a youth pastor is the key to successfully giving their kids a similar experience and, to some extent, reliving their own personal experiences.

Some parents place such a high value on having a youth pastor that they'll threaten to leave the church if you don't find someone soon. Or they just leave, without threatening. A "concerned" parent may say things like, "We're going to go to a church where our teens are valued."

REASON #6: "OUR CHURCH DOESN'T HAVE ANY YOUNG ADULT LEADERS."

In this scenario, the church says, "We want our congregation to value our teenagers, but we don't have any people young enough [read: under 50] to lead the programs" or, "We're a small church with volunteers already serving in other areas." The obvious solution, then, seems to be to hire someone outside the church to lead the youth ministry.

INSIDE THE MIND OF PARENTS

The Hidden Assumption

Many parents equate having a youth staff person with the level of commitment and support a church offers them as a family. Their feelings could be stated like this: "If you care about me as a parent and if you care about my child, you'll hire a youth pastor. If you don't have a youth staff, it must mean you don't want to meet my needs."

The Problem

Sadly, this view often is right on the money. There is, however, a growing population of churches that value students *too much* to hire a youth pastor for this reason.

While that solution may seem immensely practical in the moment, it ultimately fails to address a bigger problem within the church: Why young people choose not to attend or choose not to get involved in ministry. Hiring a youth worker under those conditions would enable the congregation to maintain an unworkable demographic—one that's unhealthy and dysfunctional. Whatever kids you reach as a result of hiring a youth pastor will almost certainly stop attending your church after high school, or when the youth pastor leaves.

REASON #7: "WE NEED TO KEEP OUR MOMENTUM."

Things are going well in the youth program. You have good participation. You want to keep the numbers and excitement up. That makes sense. But if your church needs a youth pastor on staff to maintain momentum, something's wrong. You may have situations and circumstances working against your youth ministry. Churches that depend on paid or volunteer staff for momentum are dog-paddling in the open sea. That kind of ministry can't be sustained. There must be an intervention. (We'll talk more about this in chapter 4.)

REASON #8: "WE WANT TO HAVE THE BEST YOUTH GROUP IN THE AREA."

As a consultant, I hear this proclamation too often. Maybe you've heard it in your church. It's often tossed around in the interview process. It's a good line because it sells the church's desire for greatness—and youth pastors love it.

The problem with this line of thinking is there isn't a "best" youth group in the area. There are only youth groups you hear about, and youth groups you don't hear about. Being a well-known youth group has very little to do with health or effectiveness and a lot to do with size and budget.

Your church is the best church to minister to your kids, their friends, and their families. So don't put too much stock in the cool stories your pastor friends tell about their youth ministries. Most of them aren't completely true anyway.

REASON #9: "WE WANT TO KEEP KIDS BUSY AND OUT OF TROUBLE."

Keeping kids out of trouble is a worthy goal, especially when you consider the lifelong consequences that can result from spontaneous decisions made by adolescents with too much time on their hands. The Boys and Girls Clubs of America and community recreation centers exist for this very reason.

As a pastor, you know that churches have a greater purpose: Connecting young people to their Creator and helping them live their lives in a way that honors God. Youth ministry has little to do with behavior modification, which is the real goal behind this very bad reason to hire a youth pastor.

REASON #10: "WE NEED SOMEONE TO RUN OUR YOUTH PROGRAMS."

Sustaining programs is not the point of youth ministry—or the church. It often might feel like it is, but it's not. In much the same way that churches that focus on their survival actually contribute to their demise, youth ministries that focus on keeping programs running may have one foot in the grave.

The purpose of youth programs is to connect teenagers relationally to God, to other teenagers, and to adults in your congregation. If you hire someone simply to run your programs, you need to recognize it as a symptom of a far greater problem in your church.

REASON #11: "WE'VE ALWAYS HAD A YOUTH PASTOR."

This is a touchy one. It might be in your church's best interest to take a break from having a staff person devoted to youth ministry. That would give you a chance to evaluate your situation and reflect on how your church community embraces young people and their families.

REASON #12: "WE DON'T KNOW WHAT TO DO WITH OUR EXTRA MONEY."

Your church has loads of cash and doesn't know what to do with it. If that's the case, you don't need a youth pastor, you need a youth ministry consultant.

Most of these reasons involve an external force putting pressure on you or the church to find a youth pastor. That driving need can teach you something about yourself and your church, if you explore it properly. But it's important that you understand this: Feeling rushed to hire a youth pastor is a sign that something's wrong. It's a signal that there are issues to be addressed before you embark on the hiring process.

Your church has an opportunity to move forward to a healthier place. Will you take it?

DISCUSSION QUESTIONS FOR YOU AND YOUR STAFF

1. Which reason in this chapter most accurately describes our mindset the last time we hired a youth pastor?

2. What did we learn from the experience?

3. Which of the poor reasons for hiring a youth pastor are most prevalent in our church? Explain.

4. What steps can we take to make sure our mindset is right before we hire a youth pastor?

Chapter Two

THE 35-POUND RACCOON AND AN OPPORTUNITY

There is always an easy solution to every human problem—neat, plausible, and wrong.

—H. L. MENCKEN

My kids like to shop. No, that's not right. My kids like to *buy things*. No matter what store they enter, they can find something they want. When my boys were younger and just learning to assert their desire to purchase a particular toy, book, or lollipop, they tried several strategies.

Once when my son Zach and I were in a Target store, I made the mistake of walking him past the toy aisles, where he saw a *Star Wars* puzzle he wanted. He was in the second grade, which might lead you to assume that he was small and weak.

A friend once told me that a 35-pound raccoon is as strong as a 150-pound dog and can kill it—especially if the raccoon can coax the dog into deep water. I don't know if it's true, but my friend is a senior pastor who lives in the country, in an area populated by raccoons, so I believe him.

I tell you this because I believe that a 50-pound second grader is stronger than a 200-pound man when the second grader wants a *Star Wars* puzzle. Here's what happened to me.

Zach said he wanted the puzzle.

I quietly said no, reminding him that his birthday was in a couple of months. I pointed out that he might get it then as a present.

That's not the response Zach wanted. He emphasized that he *really* wanted the puzzle—that the puzzle would make him happy. He offered to feed the family dog all week— without having to be asked—in exchange for it.

I said no.

Zach started to get impatient with my inability to cooperate with him. He said, "But DAD, you don't understand. I NEED this puzzle!"

"Son," I replied. "You don't need the puzzle; you just want it. There's a difference between a need and a…"

Zach grabbed the puzzle from the shelf and hugged it with both arms like a pro running back protecting a football while being gang-tackled for short yardage. I momentarily admired his technique and wondered if he should try out for football. But then his yelling snapped me back to reality.

"I NEED IT! I NEED IT! I NEED IT!"

I'm surprised he didn't hold it above his head with one hand and declare, in his best Charlton Heston impression, "From my cold, dead hands!" But he didn't. Instead, he held the puzzle with a viselike grip—the grip of a 35-pound raccoon.

It took a few moments, but I was able to pry the puzzle from his white-knuckled fingers. When the puzzle dropped to the ground, I had both arms around Zach from behind. That's when he went bone-less and started screaming louder.

Zach threw the worst fit he'd ever thrown—or has ever thrown since. And he threw it at the place in the store that was farthest from the front door. The raccoon was now rabid. It was time to cut my losses and leave, with my 50-pound son playing deadweight.

It's a tricky thing to carry your son while he's screaming and keep people from noticing. It's amazing how carefully you can handle a kid that heavy just so you can show the world that you aren't abusing him. Once we made it past the long line of registers, Zach found his bones again and upgraded from boneless rag doll to flailing freak-out. By the time we finally got to the car, I was emotionally exhausted.[1]

Zach felt like he needed that puzzle. I knew that to give in to his forceful demand would actually harm him in the long run. I didn't buy him the puzzle because I love him. I didn't buy him the puzzle because I want something better for him than a puzzle. Better yet, I *hope* for something better for Zach than a puzzle. I hope he'll be a person who's content, discerning, satisfied, generous, whole, disciplined, and faithful to God—with the ability to do without certain things he wants. I hope he'll live with distinction in a culture where consumerism is rampant, a culture where what you buy defines your happiness. My decision not to buy that puzzle sprang from my hopes for him. But at that moment in Target, there wasn't a lot of hope. I found myself engaged in a battle for nothing less than the soul of my son.

Today Zach doesn't use the word *need* as much as he used to. I hope it's because he's starting to recognize that certain needs can be harmful to him in the long run.

YOU DON'T *NEED* A YOUTH PASTOR

Leading a church requires a similar kind of foresight and commitment to hope. Within the church life, there are things that seem natural, normal, and completely right—things we think we need—that will actually harm us in the long run. With that in mind, let me suggest that you don't *need* a youth pastor. Let me rephrase that: A healthy church doesn't *need* a youth pastor.

The people of God did just fine for thousands of years without youth pastors ministering to their kids. It's only within the last 100 years that the concept of adolescence has developed. And youth ministry as we recognize it today has only existed for the last 40 years.

---

[1] I'd just like to say that my son Zach is great. His Target fit was a once-in-a-lifetime event. Zach is one of the most tenderhearted people I know and is becoming a wonderful young man

However, in this moment, it's very likely that your church believes a youth pastor is necessary and unavoidable. That belief can motivate you to go for a quick fix (read: short-term solution) and hire a youth pastor—or it can motivate you to grow and shape your ministry into something more healthy (read: long-term solution).

The best way for your church to become healthy is to start making healthy decisions. The long-term solution can be very difficult. It can cause a scene not unlike a second grader who throws the fit of his life in a department store. It can be emotionally taxing. It requires determination and a commitment to health. It requires generous leadership orchestrating change motivated by love, compassion, and a desire to see God's best in your community.

STOPGAP STAFFING

First Church has always considered itself to have a healthy student ministry. That is to say, the kids seem happy, and there's a satisfactory number of them involved. First Church has a track record of hiring charismatic, likeable, relational youth staff the kids really like.

Every three or four years, though, the church experiences a bump in the road that threatens the health of its youth ministry. Because of First Church's success in hiring charismatic leaders, they face the problem of larger churches hiring them away. This happens, on average, about once every three years.

When the youth pastor leaves, it creates a tremendous upheaval and puts the relationship between the students and the church in jeopardy. The youth ministry at First Church revolves around the youth pastor. Maybe you've experienced a similar problem—one that springs from a larger issue.

Our culture has become preoccupied with method and technique. This preoccupation affects us all. It's the water we swim in. It's pervasive in every aspect of our culture. TV shows teach us techniques for being better parents, better spouses, better dog owners, and better citizens. I confess that at times I've become fascinated by such programs. The pursuit of a quick fix often involves a search for just the right technique, model, program, sermon series, or undeniable guidelines for leadership.

The functional quick fix for church youth ministry over the last few decades has been to find a staff person to run the ministry. It's time for those of us in the church—especially those of us in church leadership—to acknowledge that this stopgap strategy for staffing isn't the best way.

That's not to say the stopgap method can't work. It can and does sometimes. But it's a gamble with a very high failure rate. A church finds someone to run the youth ministry; when that person leaves, that church scrambles to fill the position with another person; sometimes the new youth pastor serves the congregation for years; but when he leaves, the church falls right back into its same behavior.

When will we address this unhealthy pattern for raising our kids in the way of Christ? More personally, when will you address this pattern in your church? Stopgap solutions are detrimental to your church and to the individuals you hire to solve your problems.

When you hire a youth pastor as a stopgap measure, you functionally place your entire youth ministry on the shoulders of one staff person. Often that person...

- operates apart from the rest of the church staff.

- is not inclined to integrate with adults.

- is still struggling with maturity and identity issues of his own.

- has little or no history with you or your church.

- has a theological perspective that you know little about.

When you pursue a stopgap strategy with your youth ministry, you end up with a strategy that's youth pastor-centered. And that can present a host of problems, including these:

- Older students who were close to the old youth pastor are more hesitant to connect with the new one.

- Some older students feel abandoned by the church because of the turnover and stop attending. This is especially true if they've developed relationships with two or three other youth pastors over their lifetimes. As one high school junior said, "Why would I subject myself to that kind of loss again?"

- Students often mistake a connection to a youth pastor with a connection to the church. High school students often drop out completely upon the departure of a youth pastor they loved and were committed to. That pastor was the students' only real tie to the church.

- Students experience confusion, loss, discouragement, and alienation from the church.

- The congregation becomes dependent on the youth pastor to do youth ministry on their behalf. Many begin to believe that the spiritual nurturing of teenagers isn't their responsibility.

- The congregation develops a bad habit of outsourcing youth ministry.

- The church staff experiences increased pressure to hire the right person.

Stopgap measures are not the solution for your youth ministry.

FIRST THINGS FIRST

Before you start to think about hiring a youth pastor, you need to get your youth ministry in order. A great youth ministry requires a vigorous collaborative effort on the part of everyone in the church. And you must be involved in the process in a significant way.

Opting for a long-term solution probably won't be an easy sell to your congregation. Remember, that 35-pound raccoon (your church) is stronger than you think. But I'm guessing you've tangled with that raccoon before. And you may be reluctant to pursue a long-term solution for that very reason.

Pause for a second. Take a deep breath.

Do you feel resistance to this idea? If so, where's it coming from? Within you? Or is it an external pressure being placed on you?

The resistance to the idea is likely coming from a need. And that need is likely connected to your church's assumptions about youth ministry. The urgent need you feel pushing you toward hiring a youth pastor as soon as possible can shed light on the adjustments you need to make in your church or ministry before you hire a youth pastor.

Feeling pressure to hire a staff person is a sign that something's wrong. It's a warning light on your dashboard telling you that something needs to change. It's a signal that your church lacks something vital. Reacting to that need instead of addressing it can trigger devastating consequences within your church, the body of Christ.

A friend's church regularly has to close children's Sunday school classes because they don't have volunteers to teach them. Of the thousands of people who attend the church, few seem willing to work with children. This pattern came from a quick fix in the church's history. Early on, when Sunday school workers could not be found, the church simply hired people to cover the classes. It was a quick fix. But it cost them over the long term.

In a conversation with my friend, he said, "We started hiring people to do children's ministry Sunday school, and we've taught the congregation something we didn't intend to. Now we must retrain our church to care about kids." Today the church is attempting to retrain the congregation about its role in loving and training children. As part of that process, the church has stopped covering for people who refuse to get involved. It's a hard situation to be in. Yet it's a situation that many churches find themselves in.

By hiring a youth pastor, are you teaching your congregation something you don't intend to? Are people learning that others will take care of their kids' spiritual lives?

If you aren't willing to address the needs driving your church to find a youth pastor, your church will never reach teenagers or their families to the extent that it might otherwise. And that's the best-case scenario. At worst, your church will undermine biblical fellowship and community, continue unhealthy behaviors, and leave a wake of injured staff, parents, youth, and volunteers. Even worse, it will give kids and their parents an unhealthy understanding of the good news.

Don't settle in your youth ministry. Do the hard work and avoid stopgap solutions.

DISCUSSION QUESTIONS FOR YOU AND YOUR STAFF

1. Why are we hiring a youth pastor? Is it for one of the reasons mentioned in the previous chapter? Which reason stands out to you? Why?

2. What might be some problems we as church leaders are attempting to solve by hiring a youth pastor?

3. What opportunities are before us right now? Are we fully embracing them? Explain.

4. Is there something driving us to hurry through this process? What are some of the forces, people, and assumptions pressuring us to hire a youth pastor quickly? Are we brave enough to name them?

5. If we as a church were willing to wait to hire a youth pastor and work through a process to become healthier, what are some things we'd need to work on? In other words, how could our youth ministry be healthier?

6. Are we willing to do the work that needs to be done to prepare for success in our youth ministry?

Chapter Three

GOOD REASONS TO HIRE A YOUTH PASTOR

Once you've addressed the driving needs in your church—once you've established a healthy, churchwide model for youth ministry—you'll find there are several good reasons for hiring a youth pastor. Let's take a look at some of them.

REASON #1

Your congregation is actively taking responsibility for the youth in your church, but needs pastoral leadership in overall implementation.

In this scenario, church members recognize that the kids need them in their lives as part of the youth ministry. Likewise, church members recognize that they need kids in their lives in order to have a healthy church. Finally, the church members acknowledge that teenagers and children are their God-given responsibility—one they refuse to abdicate to a paid youth pastor.

With that framework intact, the church can seek insight, direction, and encouragement from a paid youth pastor on how to fulfill its responsibilities.

REASON #2

As the senior pastor, you're looking for a partner to implement your vision for the church. You could benefit from a youth pastor's gifts, which might include a strong cultural understanding and perspective.

In this scenario, you conclude that the church could learn from a youth pastor. You believe that you could personally benefit from having a youth pastor. You welcome the opportunity to include the youth pastor as a team player. You desire change and want to connect kids with the leadership of the church in healthy ways.

REASON #3

Your church highly values missions and outreach. And though you may or may not have young people attending your church, you're willing to hire a youth pastor to be a missionary to the teenagers in your area.

The caveat is that the youth you reach may never set foot in your church. You're hiring a missionary youth worker who may take kids to another church to connect with other adults. Your church is not trying to repopulate itself, but is giving its resources to minister to students. Your church values teenagers and brings finances to the table for reaching them, whether they attend your church or not.

This is the growing edge of youth ministry. Churches with young people and churches without are funding programs to connect with teenagers outside their church. Churches that participate in this way can impact thousands of teenagers with very little effort, because they've given up the expectation for them to come to their church buildings.

A candidate for this type of ministry would be a church with an older congregation that doesn't have the manpower to do youth work, but still views teenagers as a mission field. The church would have a strong desire to build the kingdom of God, but not necessarily its own congregation. And finally, the church would have the ability to partner with other churches and organizations.

REASON #4

You want your church to take seriously its God-given responsibility for teenagers, and you need someone who will lead this change full time.

In this scenario, the youth pastor serves as a change agent. The best candidate will probably be an older, more mature youth pastor. You need someone strong enough and experienced enough to help change the behavior patterns and habits of your church. And you need someone patient enough to help it live out its responsibility. That person will likely lay the groundwork for one of the other reasons mentioned in this list.

REASON #5

You need a partner to support parents in their roles as primary spiritual nurturers of their own teenagers. This partner's primary role will be to develop people to support parents in their ministry with encouragement and tools for discipleship.

In this scenario, instead of hiring a youth pastor to work primarily with youth, you hire a youth pastor to support parents in their ministry to their kids. The church that adopts this strategy is looking to give practical support and encouragement to the parents and teenagers in its congregation.

DISCUSSION QUESTIONS FOR YOU AND YOUR STAFF

1. Which good idea stands out to you? Why?

2. Are we hiring a youth pastor for any of these reasons? Explain.

3. Do you agree that these are good reasons for hiring a youth pastor? Why or why not?

4. Which one might fit our congregation best?

5. Is there a good alternative to one of these reasons that isn't listed? If so, what is it?

6. What's the common theme among each of these good reasons for hiring a youth pastor?

Chapter Four

CHURCH A & CHURCH B

It is no accident that most organizations learn poorly. The way they are designed and managed, the way people's jobs are defined, and, most importantly, the way we have all been taught to think and interact (not only in organizations but more broadly) create fundamental learning disabilities. These disabilities operate despite the best efforts of bright, committed people. Often the harder they try to solve the problems, the worse the results.

—PETER SENGE, *THE FIFTH DISCIPLINE*

There are two dominant, overarching reasons that churches hire youth pastors. First, there's the church that hires a youth pastor to lead the youth ministry on behalf of the congregation. I'll call that Church A. Second, there's the church that hires a youth pastor to help the church members in their ministry to students. I'll call that Church B.

Church A and Church B are not static. They're in constant flux. In other words, your church couldn't say, "We've arrived at Church B." Instead, Church A and Church B are mental maps or values that influence the trajectory of your church by affecting each decision you make.

It's important to note that youth ministry continues to change dramatically in North America and will continue to make significant shifts over the next five to 10 years. Church A and Church B are not intrinsically attached to any model for the future (or past). Church A and Church B are not simply repackaged family ministries from 15 years ago, though they could be used in such a model. Youth ministry continues to occur outside the church building, with a growing number of partnerships with organizations such as public schools, other churches, or city organizations. To confine Church A or B to a building, or a traditional youth ministry, would be to miss the point.

This is not a chapter about programming. It's about life with God and the responsibility of guiding children into adulthood with Christ. Chances are, you'll feel the urge to think exclusively about programs as you read on, but you must resist that urge or you'll be in danger of missing the point entirely.

A CLOSER LOOK AT CHURCH A

This chapter is dedicated to helping your church determine which trajectory it's on. In order to understand each trajectory, we'll look at its characteristics and common results. First, let's look at Church A, the one committed to hiring a youth pastor to lead the youth ministry.

Characteristics of Church A

Church A functions as if the ultimate responsibility for the spiritual formation of students rests on the shoulders of the youth pastor. The vast majority of churches in North America fall into this category.

If you believe that the responsibility of youth ministry should rest on the shoulders of the youth pastor, you need to make that clear to interviewees before you make your hire. Fair warning is necessary because this is a destructive ideology—destructive to your staff, destructive to your church, and destructive to the kingdom of God.

In Church A, "volunteers" help the youth pastor with the ministry. These unpaid workers view themselves as support for the youth pastor. However, it's important to note that the concept of "volunteers" is nowhere to be found in Scripture. The word implies that ministry to children and youth is optional for the average congregation member. And biblically speaking, it's not.

In Scripture, there's an unspoken context of community. In biblical times, there was a corporate or communal aspect to raising kids. It was a villagewide effort. Everyone had a part. Interestingly, when I mention this to people today, I often get a response like this: "I'm called to work in prisons—or men's ministry. Why would you demand that I work in youth ministry?" That kind of question is symptomatic of the flawed notion that youth ministry takes place exclusively in programs. Certainly everyone doesn't need to serve in youth ministry programs. But everyone *does* need to minister to youth. Similarly, everyone may not be called to be a full-time vocational missionary or to go on missions trips. But everyone *is* called to live missionally.

Church A expects the youth pastor to "delegate" programs and jobs. That expectation wrongly assumes that the responsibility for youth rests squarely on the shoulders of the paid staff person. Generals and business people delegate tasks yet remain responsible for the overall project. Youth pastors might equip or empower people to nurture teenagers, but they shouldn't delegate something that doesn't belong to them in the first place.

Church A expects the youth pastor to be present at all youth activities. In other words, the youth pastor is the hub of the youth ministry wheel. I call this the Wagon Wheel.

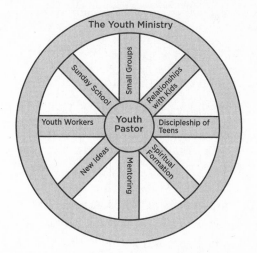

Each relationship, each program, each part of the ministry is directly dependent upon the youth pastor. Though this model is directly harmful to churches, it remains the primary way youth ministries function.

In Church A, the vision for the youth ministry comes exclusively from the youth pastor. The church may have a board (made up of parents and other adults) that advises the youth pastor, but usually it has little or no responsibility for implementing ministry to teenagers in the church. It serves principally as a resource for advice.

These boards tend to hold power but share little responsibility for implementation. The youth pastor is often held accountable by this board, but the board usually has little knowledge of what's actually happening in the ministry itself. (Boards like these are common in churches trying to solve youth pastor-related problems.)

Subtle behavior patterns are often present in Church A. And while the patterns may remain unspoken, they're communicated loud and clear to teenagers and youth workers. Those patterns include consumerism ("The church's job is to meet my needs"), abdication of responsibility ("We have our own Sunday school class to attend"), and devaluation of youth ("Young people are not equal with adults. They have needs, but adult needs are more important").

The following comments reflect the attitude of Church A:

- "We have our own jobs and families that demand our time. We need someone who can devote themselves to youth 50 hours a week."

- "I don't understand teenagers."

- "Teenagers don't want to be around adults or parents."

- "We need someone young and hip to connect with our kids."

- "We need an expert to connect with youth."

The Results of Church A

Pursuing youth ministry the "Church A way" has its consequences. One such consequence is a high rate of turnover in the youth ministry staff. One common reason for this is that the job is too large for any one person to accomplish alone. A youth pastor may shine where she's gifted, but struggle in areas of weakness. No one person can do everything it takes to make youth ministry happen. Those who try either burn out quickly, or discover it's more than they can handle and attempt to enlist support. Or they're asked to leave.

Another reason for turnover in youth ministry staff is unrealistic expectations. It's simply not possible for one individual to meet all the expectations a congregation and teenagers have for a youth ministry.

A domino effect of staff turnover is that when a youth pastor leaves Church A, many kids follow. Why? Because Church A teenagers become committed to the youth pastor instead of the church (or other ministry volunteers). Young people feel the pain of the transition but have little or no power to influence the decision. Most adults, on the other hand, experience the pain of the transition only through their kids.

In Church A, the youth pastor carries a disproportionate amount of responsibility for maintaining the youth ministry's health, organization, and programs. Volunteers have little or no ownership in the ministry. That's a problem because great youth ministry is always a team effort—not simply because it's better for the kids, but also because it's better for the staff. No one person can sustain a great youth ministry alone for a long period of time and continue to be healthy. You may have volunteers involved in your youth ministry and find yourself agreeing with my point so far. But what's interesting is that even churches with large numbers of volunteers and supporters suffer when a youth staff person elevates the programming to a level in which the staff person carries too much of the responsibility for the church's ministry to youth.

In other words, it's common to have many volunteers in your youth ministry, and still be Church A. If we look back to the Wagon Wheel illustration, we see that the youth pastor may still be the center of the youth ministry even when there are volunteers present. The number of volunteers showing up for your youth programming is not an indicator of a healthy trajectory. The ownership and responsibility for ministry (inside and outside the programs) is the way to measure health. Failure to recognize the subtle differences between the two leads many church leaders further down the destructive path of Church A. More pointedly, this is not a small church issue. It affects many of the largest churches in the country as well.

Church A youth ministry is expensive. Hiring youth ministry staff within this model can cost you kids; it can cost you time (poorly invested); and it can cost you money.

Despite these negative consequences, the Church A model for youth ministry is by far the most popular model in churches today. In fact, most church leaders accept this model as the norm. It's the only way they know how to do youth ministry. They just assume all youth pastors are transient and stay in their jobs only for a short time. They reckon that the negative consequences associated with the model are simply part of the price of doing business in youth ministry.

Though senior pastors I encounter would love to break this pattern, few know how. This model fits the Western consumer worldview, which makes it very appealing to congregations. The idea of a "full service" church where young people are spiritually nurtured by a professional is enticing to people "shopping" for a church.

The problem comes when the youth pastor leaves. Consumers have little patience for lack of service, so the senior pastor feels a significant amount of pressure to hire someone quickly to fill the gap.

There is a way to minister to youth in which the youth pastor is not the central figure in the ministry. I call this Church B.

A CLOSER LOOK AT CHURCH B

The Church B method is a far less common but more biblical approach to youth ministry. According to the Church B model, you don't hire a youth pastor to lead the youth ministry; you hire her to lead the church in its God-given responsibility to minister to adolescents and their families. As one pastor said, "We hire the youth pastor to lead us as we lead the youth ministry."

Characteristics of Church B

Church B believes the responsibility of youth ministry rests on the shoulders of the parents and the congregation. That reliance on the church family shapes every aspect of the ministry.

Generally speaking, church leaders who follow the Church B model aren't satisfied with one implementation of ministry, so they're constantly looking to make improvements. They also don't see youth ministry as an add-on to the church. They're not content with the young people being off somewhere else, out of sight. They believe teenagers are equals. Because they're in relationship with students, they begin to see the world through the eyes of their students.

In the Church B model, volunteers lead every aspect of the youth ministry while the youth pastor supports them in their God-given roles. Therefore, Church B doesn't need or expect the youth pastor to attend all youth ministry events.

Church B believes the responsibility for finding and recruiting new youth ministry volunteers rests on the shoulders of the current volunteers. What's more, the volunteers' level of involvement isn't dependent on the youth pastor. It doesn't change when a new staff person is hired.

Church B invests a significant amount of time, effort, and thought before it hires a youth pastor. The church begins its search for a youth pastor only when the time is right. There's no hurry to fill a vacancy. It's not unheard of for a Church B to wait a year or two in order to find just the right person for the job.

Though it may seem counterintuitive to some, Church B requires strong leadership from its staff. Occasionally, when I talk to church leaders about Church B, someone will assume I'm talking about building a committee or board for youth group. Leaders from mainline churches I talk to often assume they must already be doing Church B because they have youth committees. Leaders from programmatically progressive churches that have a tendency to reject formal structures of church polity initially view Church B as a big step backward from strong staff leadership.

Church B affirms the best of both worlds. Committees can be good at management, at least for short periods of time, but they often lack vision and forget why they're doing ministry in the first place. Church B requires the staff and "lay" leaders to rally around the reason the church has a youth ministry. Without great leadership, you won't move in the direction of Church B. And church leaders' worst fears of a committee-led, stagnant, and unhealthy youth ministry—one in which power is given to people who don't share the vision of the church and who will become an obstacle in the movement toward health—will come true.

The Church B model tends to foster an environment of trust among and toward its leaders. Trust and vision are its starting points. Furthermore, those involved in Church B youth ministry tend to be less reactive and exemplify less ambiguity when a staff change occurs.

Church B doesn't have a board to advise the youth pastor. Church B has a team that acts with authority and responsibility to carry out the youth ministry. They are people of action rather than opinion.

Subtle behavior patterns are often present in Church B. And while the patterns may remain unspoken, they're communicated loud and clear to teenagers and youth workers.

1. Sacrifice. To follow Christ and make disciples is, at its core, an act of sacrifice. It doesn't demand maturity of the church member, only a willingness to lay down her life for Christ. In Church A, youth ministry is based on the convenience of the people in the church. In Church B, youth ministry is marked by the sacrificial giving of people's time, gifts, and presence.

2. Innovation and Evolution. Church B is always adopting new and better ideas. Those involved in the ministry aren't content simply to maintain the status quo or do things the way they've always been done. They're constantly looking for more effective ways to make a difference in the lives of teenagers. What's more, the innovators (the people who thought of the ideas) are often the implementers (the ones who put them into practice). So nothing gets lost in the translation.

3. Youth and Adults Are Equals. That's not just lip service, though. That equality is underscored in every aspect of the youth ministry. There is no annual "Youth Service," in which the kids "get to" lead the music, take up the offering, make the announcements, and deliver a sermon—because *every* week involves students in some shape or form.

4. Reflective Leadership Composed of Learners. Reflective leaders are open to new information yet still hold strong opinions. Their lives are marked by humility and openness to the possibility of being wrong.

The phrase "leaders are learners" has been popular. And that's an admirable trait for all to aspire to. However, too often this might be translated solely as "leaders learn from experts by reading a lot of books and going to conferences." Certainly this is one way a leader can learn, but there are other ways. As a church leader, you have something to learn from everyone on your staff and in your church—believer or not, adult or not, ordained or not.

Leaders are learners not only from experts, but also from unlikely sources. It may sound simplistic, but in order to learn, a leader must be open and accessible to new information. Reading a book or going to a conference demonstrates a leader's initiative to learn. So does spending time with people with whom they often disagree. Leaders of the church must be able to reflect on what they value and believe—and make adjustments as new situations warrant.

5. Congregations Become Learning Organizations. Not only do individual church leaders need to be learning, but the communities within the church need to be as well. There's a humility in learning churches. They're not too proud to change or adapt as situations warrant.

Learning organizations are full of individuals and teams who are willing to reflect on and dialogue about practices they currently don't live out. They do this together. This is not navel-gazing, but a learned behavior in which people live and work and move toward a greater purpose in unison. Peter Senge describes a learning organization this way in his amazing work *The Fifth Discipline*: "an organization that is continually expanding its capacity to create its future." He goes on to write, "'Survival learning' or what is more often termed 'adaptive learning' is important—indeed it is necessary. But for a learning organization, 'adaptive learning' must be joined by 'generative learning,' learning that enhances our capacity to create."

The following comments reflect the attitude of Church B:

- "We aren't ready to hire a youth pastor. We have some internal issues to take care of before we'll be healthy enough for one."

- "I know you were hoping the youth pastor would do that, but that's not why we hired her."

- "I have a new way for us to accomplish our vision. Here's what I want to do, and I've already worked on our process to assemble a team." (Made by a congregation member.)

- "Let's get the youth pastor's thoughts on this before we decide we're on track."

- "We hire the youth pastor to lead us as we do youth ministry."

The Results of Church B

Generally speaking, the Church B model of youth ministry results in less staff turnover. Because the adults are invested in the ministry as much as the kids, they too feel the pain of transition. As a result, they have greater incentive to keep the youth pastor.

When a youth pastor does leave, less harm is done to the ministry in Church B than in Church A. The church itself sustains the relational core of the ministry. The day-to-day involvement of the congregation doesn't change, so the impact is less jarring to the young people.

Another result of the Church B model is a higher level of job satisfaction on the part of youth pastors. Because the churches carry the programmatic and administrative load of youth ministry, the youth pastors don't have to carry the load themselves. They don't feel the pressure to single-handedly sustain the youth ministries.

Finally, Church B offers young people a healthy understanding of what it means to follow Christ because it involves teenagers in the larger church community.

Youth ministry as we know it began in the mid-1970s. Over the last 30 years, Church A's approach to youth ministry has become entrenched in the minds of church leaders—even though it doesn't accomplish what most churches hope for.

As a youth pastor in the mid-'90s, I started to see the need for a shift toward a new kind of youth ministry. In 2000, I began to consult with churches that were trying to progress from Church A to Church B. And in June 2005, I started the Riddle Group to devote myself full time to helping churches make the difficult transition to shift their trajectory from Church A to Church B.

Sadly, there are plenty of churches that still strive for the Church A philosophy. Many church leaders prefer to pursue a youth pastor-centered model of youth ministry. Bookstores and conventions are full of resources for this approach to youth ministry. In this sense, Church A is incredibly well funded and supported. With all of the money, books, experts, conventions, and parachurch organizations that support it, Church A should work pretty well. But it doesn't. Youth pastors have known this for a long time. Senior pastors and parents are beginning to figure it out. Church A doesn't achieve the desired outcomes.

Church B is the youth ministry many church leaders wish they could have. The problem is, they don't realize it's a viable option. Church B is a different road with a different outcome. It's not perfect. It doesn't solve all of Church A's problems. In fact, it often brings its own set of problems. But more and more pastors are choosing to follow the Church B path because it's much closer to what they want for their kids, their parents, their churches, and their communities. Church B embodies life with God in that its youth ministry begins to pervade all of life as church members begin to own their unique responsibility of guiding kids in the way of Jesus.

DISCUSSION QUESTIONS FOR YOU AND YOUR STAFF

1. Which characteristics stand out to you the most in the Church A description?

2. Which characteristics stand out to you the most in the Church B description?

3. Which do you philosophically agree with most: Church A or Church B?

4. Give an example (sermons, brochures, procedures) of how we philosophically hold this position.

5. Which do you think we functionally align with more: Church A or Church B? Explain.

6. Which do we want to be: Church A or Church B? Why?

7. What will it take for us to get there?

Chapter Five

A TALE OF TWO YOUTH PASTORS

Carl and Jeff were both youth pastors in the same church. Jeff arrived one year after Carl resigned. Their stories are representative of a larger pattern within churches across North America. The majority of youth ministry staff hires usually follow one of the two following models.

THE TALE OF CARL

Before coming to the church, Carl worked with kids for a few years in a Christian camping ministry. Carl is pretty good with people, and kids really like him. If I were to introduce you to Carl today, it would be his integrity that strikes you first—and with good reason. Carl is a very good guy, with a sincere heart for God and kids. He's a servant leader with a humble heart. He also happens to be hip and cool.

However, a few adult "volunteers" in the church struggled with his organization of, and ideas for, youth programming. While Carl was told to implement his vision for youth ministry, he met significant resistance from a few key families that didn't like the changes he introduced. The vast majority of kids and families really liked Carl and thought he was doing a good job. But the key families who had a different vision for the youth ministry forced him out.

Carl was a great leader, but he didn't understand that there were landmines under the surface to navigate. He was unable to detect many of them and ultimately stepped on one too many.

THE TALE OF JEFF

Jeff is gifted, charismatic, and visionary. A strong leader, Jeff is also a people person with a great personality. He skillfully organized the youth ministry and knew how to negotiate the hidden landmines within the church.

Jeff used finesse and a genuinely contagious love for God to persuade the congregation to move through conflict and move the ministry forward. Jeff had fresh ideas and started new programs, including a small group program that was the rave of the church. Adult volunteers and staff knew he was a perfect fit for the job, and they loved working with him.

Then one day Jeff left the church for another ministry opportunity. To the casual observer, Jeff's decision looks like normal youth pastor behavior—hopping from one ministry to the next. Just another case of one organization snatching up a gifted youth pastor from another.

Let me give you some insight into a reality beneath the surface of this "normal" youth pastor move. Jeff thought the senior pastor and other key decision-makers in the church were incompetent—gutless and afraid to take chances. From Jeff's perspective as a dynamic leader, the church he served in wasn't led by people who would lay it on the line to be faithful.

Youth pastors like Jeff aren't perfect. They have a lot to learn about humility. While Jeff would've liked to stay at the church, he was unhappy most of his time there. He considered the larger ministry of the church a failure. He simply chose not to invest his energy into kids who would ultimately leave the church after they graduated anyway.

Carl was willing to stay. The youth ministry was doing pretty well under his leadership, but he was forced out because of politics.

Jeff resented the senior staff. And though the youth ministry thrived while he was there, he didn't stay.

The church leadership considered Carl to be an average youth pastor and Jeff to be a great youth pastor. In hindsight, they believe Carl was a bad choice and Jeff was the perfect fit. When Jeff left, it was his characteristics the church leaders wanted in the next youth pastor. What's interesting is that both hires produced the same result. Both men were gone within a few years—for very different reasons.

In retrospect, neither had any real chance of staying. One was great with people, but the church politics ate his lunch. The other was a strong leader, but the lack of strong leadership from the church leaders drove him crazy. Both had big strengths, whether it was integrity or vision, that also fed their weaknesses. The way they saw the world and themselves affected the way they used their gifts.

These two stories from the same church reflect most staffing situations. Both of them function within a Church A trajectory. If you want to move beyond these patterns, Church B can be helpful, but it takes some preparation, awareness, and new expectations.

DISCUSSION QUESTIONS FOR YOU AND YOUR STAFF

1. Think of youth pastors you've known over the years. Do the stories of Jeff and Carl reflect your knowledge of youth pastors' experiences?

2. Are either of these scenarios familiar to your church?

3. As a youth pastor, have you had any experiences like these?

4. What are the elements that cause these two tales to be so common?

5. What similar elements exist in our church?

6. What are ways we can develop a healthier youth staff in this regard?

Chapter Six

PREPARING YOUR CHURCH FOR A YOUTH PASTOR

Dysfunction: The only consistent feature in all of your dissatisfying relationships is you.

—DEMOTIVATOR FROM DESPAIR.COM[2]

Starting a new program is the default solution for almost every problem the church faces. Our people aren't giving? We'll do a sermon series on giving, tell more stories of stewardship in the service, and start a class on biblical money management. People aren't volunteering? We'll preach on the importance of service, tell more stories of people serving, and start a program that identifies peoples' gifts, experience, and talents, and then place them into ministry positions. And so the pattern goes.

It's time for us to recognize that these programs produce only marginal results. Though they may be occasionally helpful, programs are rarely the answer to the problems a church faces. Reliance on programs exposes the church leader's inability to see what's actually driving people to behave the way they do. Thus, the average church

[2] Despair.com is a Web site that sells "demotivators." This site mocks the motivational signs you see in the workplace. Very funny stuff. These make great gifts for youth pastors with whom you have great relationships.

often treats the symptoms of behaviors rather than the true causes. This is the essence of the quick-fix mentality.

In order to move beyond the quick-fix mentality, a church must assess its situation as objectively as possible. Only after that assessment is complete can the church move forward with an action plan. A complete assessment is especially necessary before you hire a youth pastor. Unfortunately, few churches assess their situations adequately.

To give you an idea of how to assess your church, I'll share with you how we at the Riddle Group assess a church.

1. What are three to five key strengths of the church's youth ministry? (These will likely include the strengths of the church.)

2. What are three to five key weaknesses of the church's youth ministry? (These will likely include the weaknesses of the church.)

3. What are the overall values of the church? How do they connect with modern youth ministry practices?

4. What is the church's relationship with its volunteers?

   a. Are there clearly articulated expectations of youth ministry volunteers?

   b. Do the volunteers feel supported and equipped?

   c. Are the volunteers fulfilling expectations?

   d. Are the volunteers being used in meaningful and appropriate ways?

5. What expectations does the church have regarding its youth ministry?

   a. Which of those expectations are healthy? Which ones are less than healthy?

   b. What expectations aren't formally expressed?

   c. Are those expectations clearly articulated?

   d. Which expectations need significant adjustment?

6. What expectations does the church have regarding its youth ministry staff?

    a. Who manages the expectations?

    b. Are those expectations clearly articulated?

    c. What expectations aren't formally expressed?

7. What is the behavior pattern of the congregation? How does it relate to the church's overall goal for youth ministry?

    a. What is the church's understanding and value of time?

    b. How does the church handle conflict?

    c. What does the history of the church tell us about the youth ministry?

    d. Are there systems in place to effectively manage harmful behavior? Do they work?

    e. What overarching metaphors does the church use to describe itself? How does that influence behavior in positive or negative ways?

8. What is the church's youth ministry structure? How effective is it in reaching its desired outcomes?

    a. Does the youth ministry structure reflect the values of the church in regard to responsibility, roles, authority, and teamwork?

    b. Is there a more appropriate option?

9. How would you describe the overall interconnectedness of youth programming?

    a. Is there redundancy in the programming?

    b. Is the programming achieving the desired outcomes?

    c. Is the programming able to achieve the desired outcomes?

    d. What needs to be added programmatically?

    e. What needs to be dropped programmatically?

    f. What drives each program?

10. How would you describe the financial aspect of your youth ministry?

    a.   Does the ministry receive sufficient funding?

    b.   Does the financial aspect of the ministry align with your church's values, size, and vision for the youth ministry?

We gather information for our assessment from parents (of junior high and high school kids), students (junior high and high school), church staff members, Sunday school teachers, Bible study leaders, small group leaders, additional volunteers, and congregation members. We spend extended time with people in key leadership positions, including adult volunteers, the youth pastor's supervisor, the senior pastor, the youth pastor, elders, and anyone else the church deems significant to this process.

We gather our information through one-on-one interviews with individuals; through surveys to parents, teenagers, and youth staff; and through a church history survey.

After we gather and evaluate the information, we develop a roadmap of Action Points based on the assessment. We create a game plan for moving ahead. Each piece of information is given appropriate weight during the assessment as the roadmap is developed. Then we assist the congregation in implementing the roadmap before the new staff person is hired.

The single biggest mistake most churches make in regard to their youth ministry is failing to cover the necessary ground in advance of hiring a youth pastor. Depending on the new youth pastor to make changes or assess the situation once she comes on board is an inefficient strategy.

Churches unwilling to do the hard work before hiring youth pastors demonstrate that they're either unable to assess their realities, or they don't value their youth or youth staff.

DISCUSSION QUESTIONS FOR YOU AND YOUR STAFF

1. How objective are we right now in assessing our youth ministry's health?

2. How clear are we on what needs to be done before we hire a youth pastor?

3. What might be some of our blind spots?

4. Would it be beneficial to have someone from outside the church bring a more objective perspective?

5. What do you think about the last sentence of the chapter? Do you think it's a fair statement? Why or why not?

Chapter Seven

RETHINKING THE HIRING PROCESS

The way your church hires people directly impacts your ability to keep them. The ability of your church to look at its history—to reflect upon its past interaction with youth staff—and its ability to make internal adjustments will determine how well you select your next youth pastor.

In order to assist you in this process, I offer the following self-assessment exercise. Take some time to go through the exercise by yourself and/or with your team.

SELF-ASSESSMENT: OUR HISTORY WITH YOUTH PASTORS

1. In the left column, list the names of the youth pastors your church has had over the last *20* years. (That's right—the last 20 years.)

2. In the next column, list the dates they were employed by your church.

3. In column three, list the reasons they left the position.

4. In column four, describe in detail what you remember about that era of ministry in the church and in the youth ministry. If you don't remember, ask others. List the big events and circumstances that occurred during that time.

5. In column five, write one-word descriptions of the climate of the church and youth ministry at the end of each person's time on staff. For example, was there hostility toward the staff—especially the youth pastor?

6. In the final column, ask yourself if you're remembering all the details objectively. Make sure you aren't rationalizing how things went down. Are you facing all of the hard, brutal facts?

Name	Dates on Staff	Reason for Leaving	Events and Circumstances That Marked This Era of Ministry	Climate	Are We Really Being Honest about This?

Do you see any patterns in your responses? What does this information tell you about how you've hired in the past? What's at the root of the behaviors or values you see represented, whether good or bad?

Now that you're beginning to think about what makes you tick as a church, we can look at common ways in which youth pastors are hired.

A BROKEN PROCESS

The first key to an effective candidate search is recruiting the right people for your search team. The common practice for assembling a search team is to choose random people from different demographics in the church—parents with middle school kids, parents with high school kids, a youth ministry volunteer, a board member or two, plus a couple of kids from the youth ministry.

This strategy is occasionally the result of a senior pastor looking to avoid blame for a bad hire. More often, it is the result of a senior pastor who knows only this way to hire a youth staff. The pastor creates a focus group of sorts to select the youth pastor. And though it's a common practice, it rarely works. The committee members may be great folks, but if they hold no power to manage the expectations for the candidate or her ministry after she's been hired, it will likely create a significant breakdown in the future.

Interviewing in this way is confusing for everyone involved, especially the youth pastor. The idea is that the assembled team is a representation of the people in the congregation and that they can articulate what the church really wants. This is rarely the case, however. And even if it were, it would still be a broken system. Staffing by democracy—or focus group—is not even close to the best-case scenario.

The youth pastor candidate believes that the search team speaks for the congregation, even though the team may hold no real authority in the church (with the exception of hiring this one particular staff person). Moreover, there are no means of communicating to the candidate to what extent the people interviewing her are correct in their assessment of the church's health and its response to, for example, crisis. The fact is most of the team members probably have very limited experience with how the church actually works and handles such things. As a result, the candidate gets a warped or limited view of what the church is really like, from a group of people who hold little authority to support the youth pastor once she's hired.

TIME

It's remarkable how little time the average church invests in the process of hiring a youth pastor. Take a look at the following interview history of one youth pastor who's been in ministry for 12 years.

One Youth Pastor's Interview History

Church #1

The senior pastor of a small church took the youth pastor candidate to lunch. That was followed by a 45-minute conversation. The senior pastor talked to one of the candidate's references for less than 10 minutes. The senior pastor called the candidate the next day to offer her the job.

Total Time Spent Interacting with the Candidate: *2 hours*

Church #2

She interviewed with a midsized church. She had one phone conversation that lasted 45 minutes and another that lasted 40 minutes. She then had an interview with the search team that lasted 60 minutes. At the end of the interview, she was asked to step into the hall for a few minutes. Five minutes later, she was invited back into the room and offered the job on the spot.

Total Time Spent Interacting with the Candidate: *2 hours and 25 minutes*

Church #3

A large church's executive pastor interviewed her for 60 minutes. She was then invited to the church for a weekend that included

    a. a 55-minute lunch with the senior pastor and a church board member;

b. 90 minutes with the executive pastor;

c. a 90-minute interview with the search team;

d. 90 minutes with other youth ministry staff.

A week after the visit, the executive pastor called to offer her the position.

Total Time Spent Interacting with the Candidate: *6 hours and 25 minutes*

Church #4

The senior pastor of a large church and the staff committee interviewed her for 55 minutes. The senior pastor admired the youth ministry of Church #3, and someone on the staff team knew the candidate. The senior pastor called the candidates' three references and talked with them less than 15 minutes each. The senior pastor called two days later to offer her the job.

Total Time Spent Interacting with the Candidate: *55 minutes*

Church #5

This church had the most comprehensive interview process. First, the church had the candidate fill out a questionnaire and an application. After that, she had an initial 25-minute conversation with a staff member. A week later, she had a 30-minute conference call with three members of the staff committee.

The church then flew her in for two days. The leadership pastor and his wife took the candidate and her husband out to dinner and then drove them to the hotel (2 hours). The next morning, the leadership pastor picked up the candidate and her husband and showed them parts of the city (90 minutes). The candidate then had lunch with the church's executive team (90 minutes). She attended a backyard dinner with a group of church leaders (3 hours). She visited an elder's house (90 minutes). She spoke Sunday morning for the middle school group (30 minutes) and the high school group (30 minutes). She finished the visit with an interview with the search team (90 minutes).

The church flew her out again for another two-day visit that included an interview with the search team (90 minutes), a meeting with elders (60 minutes), a meeting with the staff (60 minutes), and a meeting with the students (60 minutes). The church offered her the job a week after the second visit.

Total Time Spent Interacting with the Candidate: *17 hours and 25 minutes*

Working an average of 55 hours a week, this youth pastor logged approximately 32,340 hours of ministry for five churches over the course of 12 years (figuring in vacation time). And those churches took a grand total of 29 hours and 10 minutes to get to know her before hiring her.

Do those numbers surprise you? Does that process seem ideal to you? Is there any wonder why the turnover rate in youth ministry is so high?

Filling a position of such importance in the life of a church should involve spending as much time as necessary getting to know a person before you make a staffing decision. Youth pastors and churches often develop rocky relationships because, as time passes, they unearth things about each other they don't like—things that were present before their relationship began but neither knew about. Those discoveries often end ministry relationships.

Of course, there may be issues that arise later—a moral failure, for example—that end the relationship. But you can save yourself a lot of trouble by taking the time to discover personality issues, chemistry, and philosophies of ministry before you invite someone to join your staff.

The next person you hire as a youth pastor will spend countless hours with the teenagers and families of your church. Moreover, this is the person Church A will trust to spiritually form their children. In Church B, this individual will be responsible for leading adults and teenagers along in their faith. In both circumstances, the goal is to hire someone who will develop friendships that last a lifetime. The selection of this person carries a certain amount of gravity. The outcome a church hopes for in its youth ministry is often short-circuited by the way it hires new staff.

A LONG VIEW OF STAFFING

My friend Andy leads a large church with several hundred teenagers attending its midweek program. As of this writing, the church doesn't have a paid youth pastor and isn't in a hurry to find one.

Andy has a long view toward hiring a youth pastor and a high view of God's sovereignty. He runs into all kinds of people in the community—youth pastors from other churches among them—at beer-league softball games, high school football games, and the like. He receives introductions through mutual friends. He builds friendships with people he likes.

The idea of a pastor meeting youth pastors from other churches in his community might feel wrong to you. Perhaps you perceive that Andy is a looter, looking to steal another church's staff. Quite the contrary: Andy is just friendly. You might also consider that Andy isn't really looking for a youth pastor. Most of the time, youth pastors find him. And since Andy isn't in a hurry to fill his staff position, he rarely thinks about people he meets as being potential staff members.

Imagine having a youth pastor position available in your church but not having to think about it all the time.

Occasionally Andy encounters a youth pastor he connects with. If he likes the person, he'll take the youth pastor to lunch—because that's what friends do. Remember, Andy isn't trying to fill a position. He's building a friendship and testing the waters of relationship. He's asking basic questions about chemistry. That's what friends do.

As of this writing, Andy's church has been without a youth pastor for more than 20 months. The youth ministry is growing kids spiritually and numerically and expanding its programs to meet the diverse needs of the kids in the community. And all of this is taking place in a church that traditionally doesn't have a tremendously reliable volunteer base.

Andy invites friends to speak to the kids or train his youth workers. When the church decides it's ready to fill the youth pastor position, he'll look first to one of those friends—someone he knows, someone he's seen interact with his youth leaders, someone he thinks might be a good fit for the church. Then he'll invite that person into the interview process.

This is a long view of staffing—with relationships, chemistry, and philosophy at the heart of it. By the time Andy hires a youth pastor, he's talked sports, family, and politics (church and state) with that person. He's given and received feedback. He's "done life" with that person.

I'm not saying you need to take 20 months to hire a youth pastor. I'm only suggesting that there's a way your church leaders can get to know your next youth staff person before she starts working for you. Likewise, the youth pastor candidate can get to know you and your church. I'm sure Andy has friends who could never work with him. By taking the long view of staffing, you give them an opportunity to find that out and then make an informed decision.

If you're going to hire a youth pastor, you need to invest a significant amount of time into getting to know who that person is and what makes that person tick. That investment would represent not only a change in the way a youth pastor is hired, but also a change in the relationship between the youth pastor and senior pastor.

In a technological world, there are few reasons why people can't connect and get to know each other over a long period of time. Applications such as Skype, SMS, and email make connection and communication easy, even over long distances.

The way you hire staff for your youth ministry will impact how you keep a youth pastor. If you simply can't overhaul the interview process, at the very minimum (as a senior pastor) you might consider spending a couple of days with a serious youth ministry candidate. Talk about faith, movies, family, philosophy of ministry, Church A and Church B, the role of parents in ministry, hopes you both have regarding your working relationship, and how success will be measured. Try to unearth hidden assumptions you and the candidate have about youth ministry and its role within the church.

One thing is clear: The process must change so that interviewers and interviewees alike can make more informed decisions. Rethinking the hiring process can have a tremendous impact on your church's youth ministry. It can save you and your future staff a lot of heartache as well.

HOW TO FIND A YOUTH PASTOR

A few years ago I was talking to members of a search team on the phone about their search for a youth pastor. Toward the end of our conversation, I asked this question:

"After you've talked to all the candidates you're interviewing, how will you know which one is the right one for your church?"

The chairman of the committee quickly responded. "We will know because we trust God to show us. We'll just know it when we meet that person."

I paused for a moment and then rephrased the question. "I'm glad you are trusting God to bring you the right person," I said. "That's a very good thing to do. Tell me, how will you know when the person God has put before you is the one?" At that point I was resisting the urge to mention lights from heaven over the candidate or a halo hovering over the person's head.

I continued. "In this conversation, each of you has expressed expectations for the youth pastor. Some team members' expectations are in conflict with those of other team members. I'm wondering if you can put words to the characteristics of a candidate you will get excited about."

There was a long pause at the other end of the line. I began to wonder if I'd lost my connection. I could tell it was a question they wanted to answer but weren't sure how.

TRUST GOD AND DO THE WORK

As you search for a youth pastor, continue to trust God to bring you the right person for your church *and* do the hard work of personal discovery in advance. Don't let enthusiasm over a personal issue cloud your thinking on this. One way to bring clarity to your church is to develop a profile of the potential candidate. Make it realistic. What kind of experience does the next youth pastor need to have? Compare your hopes with the values of your church.

Simply asking God to show you who your next candidate is without doing the hard work of developing a profile is nothing more than laziness, lack of experience, or a combination of both. If God knows who your next youth pastor is, trust God to let you in on the details in advance. It's roughly the equivalent of the pastor who refuses to prepare for a sermon and says, "God will give me the words." God certainly does that at times. Of course, God might give you the words in advance as well. And it's likely that the prepared words may be more articulate than a spontaneous sermon. Preparation always allows for greater spontaneity.

When you spiritualize your search, you set yourself up for potential problems, such as the development of an overly emotional connection with certain candidates. But the most common problem relates to hiring the most eloquent candidate. As a result, most churches hire the best interviewee rather than the best fit for the ministry. There are some great interviewees out there looking for youth ministry jobs, but I'd never hire them as a youth pastor in my church. Having the right answer spoken in just the right way in a moment of time is very different from leading a group of teenagers and their families in their spiritual lives. Thinking through what you're looking for in a candidate keeps you from jumping the gun and hiring the wrong person.

Remember there are way more youth pastors who don't fit your church than do. And an interview isn't the ideal tool for telling the difference.

GOD DID THIS? REALLY?

Spiritualization can take many forms in church staffing situations. One that impacts youth ministry is blame. Sometimes churches unintentionally blame God for staff departures. God may have called your youth pastor somewhere else, but the fact that your church's parent council called every family in the church to slander the youth pastor's character didn't help keep him on staff.

It might surprise you how often our consultants hear this kind of rhetoric: "God called our youth pastor to another church." "We keep training youth pastors, and God keeps calling them to other churches." If I may be so bold, allow me to say this: Don't blame God for the high turnover rate of your church staff.

The same advice applies to youth pastors who pass blame by saying, "God is telling me to leave." This attempt to spiritualize our dysfunctions—our lack of satisfaction with our situations or our inability to recognize our poor choices—only hurts people in God's name. Perhaps a more appropriate explanation would be, "It's time for me to leave—to go someplace where I can serve God in a way more in line with how I'm gifted and what I feel called to do." That kind of response lets you own the responsibility for the move.

Of course, there are churches that process information and conflict through spiritualization. My friend Mitch was a youth pastor in a church that suffered from chronic anxiety. During a time of conflict, a man named Russ, who was a significant nonprofit ministry leader in the city, left the church. Though Russ didn't have any kids in the youth group, he stated in a letter to Mitch's elders that the youth ministry was the reason he was leaving the church.

Mitch didn't really know Russ, so it surprised Russ when Mitch called him regarding his letter. Mitch was hoping to learn something from Russ and pinpoint his concerns about the youth ministry. Toward the end of the phone call, Russ said, "Look, Mitch, I don't have a problem with you or the youth ministry. God is just telling me to leave. I've prayed about it a lot, and I'm sure that God wants our family to go somewhere else. Mitch, I want you to know that I didn't want to leave. I love this church and would never want to leave. But God wants me to, so I have to." Not surprisingly, when Mitch got off the phone, he had a hard time processing what he'd heard.

WHY DOES GOD KEEP TAKING MY YOUTH PASTOR AWAY?

There are times when God calls people to do things they don't want to do. But the rhetoric of blaming God for our own issues goes against the very nature and cause of Christ and his kingdom. Until churches recognize that this kind of talk is teaching something other than kingdom values to their teenagers, they may inadvertently cause spiritual damage with their staffing issues.

Imagine a 14-year-old student who keeps hearing that God is leading his youth pastor away. One student summed it up when she asked, "What kind of God would keep doing that? Can't God find someone who will stay longer? Maybe there's something wrong with us [the students] that's upsetting God."

Spiritualized rationalization isn't simply bad theology; it's a way church leaders corporately lie to themselves. If church leaders can explain away the reasons they can't keep youth pastors for long and somehow blame it on God, then they don't have to face the reality that, as leaders, they're part of the problem and have some behaviors to change.

THEOLOGY AND STAFFING

The staffing solutions I described earlier in the book as Church A and Church B are theological in nature. My experience is that most church leaders focus their theology on epistemology, but their ecclesiology often doesn't reflect what they believe. In other words, pastors often have strongly held beliefs but lack the experience or competency to practice what they preach when it comes to how the church functions.

As a result, they look to business models, popular "leadership" speakers, and the like for staffing suggestions. I suggest that this is a truly horrifying turn of events, and its effects on the church have been painful and divisive.

America's churches need leaders who think about the practical application of their theology—and find ways to equip their people to do the same. It's my contention that staffing is theological in nature. I'm not talking about a rigid, systematic kind of theology, where we continue the nonsense of developing hard and fast definitions of elder, deacon, youth pastor, music director, and so forth. I'm saying that our understanding of community, humanity, the relationship of the church to culture, and the role of the church impacts the way we staff. I'm suggesting that you allow what you believe of God and the church to influence your staffing decisions more than past procedures or current business models. Certainly business can have its place in the church, but it must always be secondary to theological belief.

In fact, your staffing preferences expose your theology. Lead a discussion among your church leaders to see where your staffing ideas and theology intersect. That way you'll be able to develop a better understanding of the role of staff in your church.

LOOKING FOR A YOUTH PASTOR? GOOD NEWS! EXPECT IT TO TAKE A WHILE

There are a lot of people looking for youth pastor jobs, but very few who fit your church. It's easy to find quality candidates who aren't a match for your church. Chances are, though, you won't be able to tell the difference between a great candidate and a potential match simply by looking at a résumé, talking on the phone once, and then conducting an interview over the weekend.

Finding the right person for your church will take some time—and that's a good thing. The longer it takes, the more opportunity your church members have to own the ministry themselves. The waiting period gives them a chance to develop a vision, prepare for the new staff member, and implement your roadmap.

Remembering the opportunities that waiting affords will help you maintain a good attitude about the search. That may not be the case for everyone, though. Some disconnected people in your church may not understand why you're taking so long. But each time someone wants to rush you to find a staff person, you have an opportunity to reinforce the fact that you and your church value teenagers—and that your church is choosing to live out healthy values. Waiting also gives you the opportunity to watch people in your church lead—and that may result in what some folks call the "farm team" approach to staffing.

THE FARM-TEAM APPROACH

Is there someone in your church who's already doing the job of a youth pastor? Is there someone in your church who's a proven leader, with a heart for kids, who might be a fit for the job? Is there someone in your ministry who has the potential to do the job? Hiring from within is the farm-team approach to staffing.

Advantages of the Farm-Team Approach

The farm-team approach is an increasingly popular option for staffing that offers a lot of advantages. Let's take a look at a few of them.

1. You know the person fits your church.

It's not uncommon for a youth pastor to confess that she wouldn't attend the church she works for if she weren't on staff. Your youth pastor needs to fit the unique DNA of your church. It's difficult to teach DNA to a new staffer. People within your church already know how your church works and what it values. Hiring someone from within helps ensure a DNA match. Finding someone who's already committed to your local church community is a benefit that can't be minimized.

2. You know the person is committed to your church and its vision.

When you hire someone from outside your church, you take a risk. You assume the candidate you select will be committed to your church, but you have no guarantee. However, when you see someone in your church serving without pay, week in and week out, there's no question about commitment. The people in your church choose to attend your church. They show their commitment by their very presence.

3. You know who the person really is.

When you hire from the farm team, you're hiring a known quantity. To know a person's character and how she responds to crisis, all you have to do is pay attention. You've served beside the person. You know who she is. You've seen her in action. Hiring someone from outside the organization presents a higher risk in this area.

Disadvantages of the Farm-Team Approach

Of course, there are some drawbacks to the farm-team approach to staffing. Let's take a look at a couple of them.

1. The person will likely lack experience and insight.

A candidate from the farm team will likely have significantly less experience than a candidate from outside your church. The person will lack insight gained from past experiences, which will likely result in some mistakes in the short run. Because the in-house candidate lacks experience, he will likely tend to manage the youth ministry rather than lead it. That problem can be overcome by picking a person with leadership qualities and coaching him to realize his potential.

2. The person will likely lack certain skills.

Another disadvantage to hiring from the farm team is that the person will likely not possess some of the skills you'd see in a candidate from the outside. Of course, farm-team advocates will remind us that skill can be taught more easily than DNA or character.

Chapter Nine

A REALLY BAD INTERVIEW QUESTION

"What's your vision for youth ministry?"

It's a question every youth pastor has learned to answer. It's the equivalent of asking, "If you get the job, what are you actually going to do?"

Some churches ask the vision question as a way of finding clues to the candidate's dreams. Other churches are looking for specific plans for the future. "We will do three mission trips a year, start small groups in the fall, and have a big outreach event every month."

Vision is a buzzword these days. It seems like a word church leaders should know and use. In fact, you probably have. Think about it. Have you ever said something like, "We're looking for a youth pastor with a vision for youth ministry"? It can seem like a good idea. But be aware: This phrase can cause tremendous confusion and widespread problems as you search for a youth pastor—especially for churches that don't already have a clear understanding of their own vision and values for youth ministry.

WHAT THE YOUTH PASTOR HEARS

When a church asks, "What's your vision?" the candidate usually receives it in one of two ways. First, she may assume you'll thoroughly compare and contrast your detailed vision and values with hers—and won't offer her the position unless her vision is compatible with yours. But frankly many churches don't have a vision for youth ministry they can clearly articulate among their own leadership—let alone use that vision as a standard in the hiring process. This often leads to conflict down the road. When the youth pastor implements her vision and gets serious congregational resistance, she'll learn the hard way that her assumption was a faulty one. This is what Carl assumed in the story from chapter 5. He didn't see the unexpressed vision until he inadvertently crossed purposes with a few volunteers. Jeff, on the other hand, intuitively perceived what people were saying and massaged the situation.

Alternatively, she may assume she's getting a blank slate—complete freedom to create a youth ministry program according to *her* vision. In the interview process the youth pastor hears, "We don't have a vision; bring yours." And often that's exactly what the church thinks it wants—for the youth ministry expert to come in and show the church how youth ministry is done. At least that seems to be the case until the new youth pastor unknowingly smashes one of the church's sacred cows.

In both scenarios, the youth pastor and the youth ministry are set up for conflict. In both instances it's because the new youth pastor assumes the church is on board with her vision for ministry when, in fact, it isn't.

A HARSH REALITY

These conflicts are often due to the fact that the church actually *does* have strong ideas concerning what the youth ministry should look like—even if a formal vision for youth ministry has never been articulated. And though it's not clear in their minds, church members often have very firm values in place as to what should and shouldn't happen in a youth ministry. What's more, your church probably has several expectations for youth ministry but can only clearly communicate one or two of them. But please understand: A potential youth pastor cannot be expected to know your church's unarticulated values for ministry. Oh, you can be sure he'll eventually find them—usually after stumbling over them and causing conflict in the process. The best way to avoid this kind of conflict is to clearly communicate your church's values in the interview process—before you hire a youth pastor whose vision and values are incompatible with those of the church.

The problem is that most churches aren't adequately reflective or self-aware to clearly identify and articulate most of their own values. So the people on the search team don't have a clear idea of what they're looking for in a candidate.

Churches by and large are only superficially reflective when it comes to organization. Many don't think about these issues at all. Churches need to be learning organizations—organizations that can take a step back and see the big picture over time and understand their mission from that perspective.

This myopia is most evident in the wake of conflict with the previous youth pastor. That person's mistakes unintentionally identified a value the church strongly holds (i.e., the youth pastor crossed a previously unidentified value and created a problem). As a result, the church will know to communicate that value to the next candidate. It was identified for them through conflict.

Most churches are looking for a youth pastor who's not the person they had before. And while it's very important to understand what bugged you about the previous youth pastor, odds are you'll get a pendulum swing despite your best efforts. Few churches take the time to decompress from one youth pastor and spend significant time drawing out their vision from within the church itself—which is always the healthiest way to determine your vision and values for ministry.

As a result, a church will often make a hiring decision based on who held the position most recently. If the previous youth pastor was gifted relationally but poor administratively, odds are good that the next youth pastor will be a good administrator—even though relationships might suffer. And on it goes.

Don't let the gravitational pull of your past influence your future. If you react against what happened before, you'll taint what is to come. So take the time now to discover what your church values. Then when you're ready to hire a youth pastor, you can discover what the candidates value. Remember, your church is simply looking for someone who values what you value.

Chapter Ten

BEFORE YOU SAY YES: A CHAPTER FOR YOUTH PASTORS

Doing your homework before you join a church staff will save you a lot of heartache later. The better you educate yourself about how things work within the church, the better your chances will be for job satisfaction.

The following principles are not necessarily reasons to avoid certain churches; they are tools for understanding churches more fully. However, you may find that after learning more about the inner workings of a particular church, you choose to say no.

Consider this scenario:

First Church is hiring a youth pastor. During the interview process, you discover the church wants the new youth pastor to start no later than 60 days from now.

As you weigh the decision, there are two principles you need to consider.

PRINCIPLE #1: A HEALTHY CHURCH ISN'T IN A RUSH TO HIRE A YOUTH PASTOR

When a church is in a hurry to hire a youth pastor, it's a sign that something is wrong. If you learn to read the signs, you can educate yourself on what you're getting into. A healthy church can wait indefinitely for a new youth pastor. If it takes a year, the church can wait. If it takes three years, the church can wait.

Hurry is a sign that something is wrong, because it suggests pressure from within the organization to take action more quickly than it naturally would. If, for instance, there's a pressure to hire a youth pastor soon out of fear that students will stop coming, then you can read the sign that says, "The youth pastor is the center for all relationships with kids in our church, and we don't have enough volunteers."

If there's a pressure from parents to find a youth pastor, you can research the origins of it by asking questions about what kind of leader the senior pastor is and what kind of authority parents have in making day-to-day decisions in the church.

Youth pastors and churches who take their time in the hiring process to get to know each other are more likely to be a healthy fit.

PRINCIPLE #2: YOU DON'T WANT TO BE SOMEONE ELSE'S RUSHED DECISION

Never accept a youth ministry job immediately after being offered it. Take some time. This isn't about playing hard to get; it's about making a good decision. Take anywhere from a week to a month to think and pray about it.

You want to be careful, though, not to lead a church on. If you have no intention of accepting a position, don't wait 30 days to let the church know. The church is honoring you by giving you time to make your decision. Don't abuse it.

If you feel pressure to give an answer more quickly, reflect on why you feel that way and where the pressure is coming from. Once you start to identify what's motivating a church, you can begin to ask questions in a humble, nonthreatening way. View yourself as a consultant and see what various church leaders think about the issues you've identified. See if there's more to the story. That kind of investigation will help you make a more informed decision. Churches (and people) want to put their best foot forward. And there's nothing wrong with that. As a candidate, though, you want to look beyond the surface. You want to find out how decisions are made, who holds the power, and who feels the pressure in day-to-day situations. Learning those things helps you get a dose of reality as to what it's really like on staff.

QUESTIONS TO ASK YOURSELF BEFORE YOU TAKE A YOUTH MINISTRY JOB

Every interview situation is unique. And every job has its benefits and its drawbacks. As you evaluate a ministry opportunity, here are some questions to ask yourself.

How do the senior pastor and other church leaders handle pressure?

Is there significant anxiety among the leadership and staff?

Is there a climate of trust or a climate of worry in the church?

Is there a lot of talk about "how we're going to convince people of new ideas"?

Is there a lack of people willing to step up and lead?

In order to get the answers you're looking for, you may need to ask questions about how past conflicts and confrontations were handled—and about how critical issues were addressed.

Do I like the person who will be my supervisor?

Is the supervisor the kind of person you get along with?

How does the supervisor's personality compare with yours?

What are the chances that your supervisor will change?

How does the supervisor handle conflict?

Will the supervisor redirect criticism to you?

Does the person have a history of being hard on the people she supervises?

How will your performance be measured?

How often will you meet with your supervisor?

Do I like the senior pastor—as a teacher and as a person?

What kind of access will you have to the senior pastor when you're on staff?

What kind of access did you have during the interview process? (That may be an indicator of how much access you'll have later.)

Are you theologically in the same ballpark as the senior pastor?

Do the two of you value similar things?

What does the senior pastor expect from you?

Is it possible to schedule extended time with the senior pastor each year?

Does the church have a learning disability?

Does the church learn from its mistakes?

Does the church have a history of remembering its values?

Is the church reflective?

Does the staff read many books?

Does the staff empower nonstaff people to be a part of the change process?

Does the church have a history of genuine dialogue?

Do people listen?

Is there a commitment to communication?

How fast does change occur within this church?

What assumptions are at play in this process?

What assumptions do you have about your role?

What assumptions do you have about the purpose of the youth ministry?

What assumptions do the people you talk to have about the role of the youth pastor and the youth ministry?

How do I feel about the interview process?

Why does the church conduct its interview process this way?

Does the church seem in a hurry to fill the position? If so, what's the rush? Where's the pressure coming from?

Do I have chemistry with the staff and key leadership of the church?

Are these your type of people?

Do you know where they're coming from?

Is there an intersection between your greatest hopes for the church and the leaders' past actions?

Are there any areas in which you've needed to convince yourself that this is going to work? Is there anything you've forced yourself to overlook in order to persuade yourself that this is a good fit?

Do you spend your spare time doing some of the same things the staff spend their spare time doing?

Are you influenced by the same pastors, leaders, books, music, movies, and theologians?

Asking great questions often leads to more questions. So when you're candidating for a position, you don't have to have *all* your questions answered. But asking many of these questions will give you a better understanding of the kind of people and system your future may involve. Questions open the doors to understanding the way a church thinks and acts. How a church responds to these questions will tell you a lot as well. Some of these questions will be difficult for a church to answer—and that in and of itself is an answer of sorts. Churches that discourage you from asking a lot of questions are letting you in on something as well.

Carving out space for better understanding a church is your responsibility as the candidate. It's up to you to establish how you want to get the information. It may feel uncomfortable at first. But the more informed you are, the fewer surprises you'll encounter once you're on staff.

Chapter Eleven

CATALYTIC LEADERSHIP

---

ce of the
lak
ters
to
is
nks to
r many
ves
lot
i.
o safety
doned if
escaping
ver be

ety

have their favo..... causes to cite,
although many of these raise the
further question of why they have

students uo ....y!

..iot by phone. We may edit letters,
which must be exclusive.

..c mucr
spread."
Pinner, Mi

She k

Sir, So I
Sadler-S
whether
than men
August 15
Had th
he woul
QUENT
West i

DIRECTOR OF STUDENT MINISTRIES

Seeking a catalytic leader to develop and administer all facets of student ministries for grades 6-12, focusing primarily on small groups, Bible studies, discipleship and leadership. Must be a leader of leaders with incredible administrative skills. Must have large-church experience (1,500+). Application deadline May 15. Immediate, full-time position offering competitive salary and benefits. If you've been yearning for a healthy environment, please submit your resume today, with cover letter including salary history.

If you read the job postings for church staff positions, you'll find that many churches are looking for strong leaders for their student ministries. They say things like, "Wanted: Catalytic leader," or "Wanted: Dynamic, creative leader." These churches want a catalytic leader for the rapid change and creativity such people can produce. Church leaders love innovation—especially when the church down the street starts doing creative stuff.

It's important to understand, though, that most churches aren't really looking for leaders, let alone catalytic leaders, to steer their youth ministries. Sure, they may say they want strong leadership, but they don't consider the implications of actually hiring strong leaders. Having a strong leader on staff can cause serious disruption to the status quo. Many churches don't want dynamic leaders in youth ministry because those churches have functioning values that are the antithesis of what a leader like that brings to the table. Let's look at what a catalytic leader does.

A catalytic leader causes reactions. He shakes the status quo. She thinks radically different thoughts and lives a radically different life. He's already given himself permission to think beyond the ordinary, so he often says things that challenge the very foundations of your philosophy of ministry. By her very nature, this dynamic leader cannot accept things for how they currently are. Every fiber of her being causes her to uproot, analyze, dissect, innovate, and press toward a better way of doing ministry.

Though this leader may have a healthy understanding of teamwork, she often creates problems. She rocks the boat. She occasionally fights to make a point or to expose poor thinking among other team members. Sometimes she does it with finesse, other times with brutal honesty. No matter how she does it, though, it causes a reaction. That's what a leader does. A catalytic, creative, and driven youth pastor will not stop her critique—or limit her dreaming to the youth department. And she doesn't understand why you'd want her to.

Many church staff teams value stability, status quo, harmony, and quaint discussions. Catalytic leaders challenge all of these things. They are compelled toward an ever-changing status quo. Instability is the natural habitat of the catalytic leader. That's why most churches don't really want to hire catalytic youth pastors. And frankly, it's why most catalytic youth pastors probably don't want to work for your church.

Most churches want the *fruit* of catalytic leadership, but they want it delivered in a calm, stable, harmonious, quaint, and uneventful environment. Unless you thrive on disequilibrium and constant questioning—both of which can be very effective agents of change—don't hire a catalytic youth pastor.

Your church might be better off hiring someone who's a good manager—someone who can creatively solve problems and come up with an occasional out-of-the-box idea inspired by the church down the street.

That being said, a church that does desire catalytic leadership—and can systemically sustain it—is an exciting place to work and expand the kingdom. If you decide that your church is hardwired for catalytic leadership, then there's work to be done before you hire this person. You need to make sure that the people in your church understand what's coming. Communicate your church's commitment to change and get key leaders on board before the new youth pastor arrives. This sets up both the church and youth pastor for success.

DISCUSSION QUESTIONS FOR YOU AND YOUR STAFF

1. What's your assessment of the author's thoughts on catalytic leadership?

2. What's been our experience with strong leaders?

3. What kind of leader is each of us on staff? How might that be a contributing factor to some of the tension among us?

4. What would we need to do to prepare for a catalytic leader on our staff?

5. Does our staff appreciate catalytic leadership? Why or why not?

Chapter Twelve

WHAT IS THE IDEAL AGE FOR A YOUTH MINISTRY CANDIDATE?

I know I'm not going to win many friends under 25 with this argument, but older is better where youth pastors are concerned. The older your youth pastor is, the better your chances of developing spiritually mature students.

Recent studies have shown that adulthood doesn't begin until 26 years of age. This means that adolescence has been expanded to the age of 25. While this certainly has an impact on the way churches do youth ministry, it has a more immediate impact on who your church hires.

Dr. Jeffery Arnett, author of *Emerging Adulthood: The Winding Road from Late Teens through the Twenties* (not to be associated in any way with the emerging church), calls late adolescence between the ages of 18 and 25 "emerging adulthood." He identifies five main features of this stage of life:

1. It's the age of identity explorations, of trying out various possibilities, especially in love and work.

2. It's the age of instability.

3. It's the most self-focused age of life.

4. It's the age of feeling in-between, in transition, neither adolescent nor adult.

5. It's the age of possibilities, when hopes flourish, when people have an unparalleled opportunity to transform their lives.

Emerging adults certainly play an important role in youth ministry. Working within a local church could help them explore their identities and their vocational possibilities. The church should foster that kind of environment for them.

If, however, you choose to hire an emerging adult to lead your youth ministry, you must give significant attention to mentoring that person in leadership and discipleship. Teenagers need their youth pastors to have a strong sense of who they are, based on life experiences. They need youth pastors who have a sense of stability in their identities.

Certainly there are men and women in their early to mid-20s who fit the bill, but they are few and far between. Church leaders need to dispel the myth that younger is better for youth ministry leadership. It's simply not true. In fact, entrusting the spiritual leadership of your teenage children to someone who's still working through the five characteristics we listed earlier is irresponsible.

DISCUSSION QUESTIONS FOR YOU AND YOUR STAFF

1. What stands out most to you in this chapter?

2. Looking back at our previous youth pastors, did any of them have any of the five main features of emerging adulthood?

3. In what ways does this chapter directly impact us?

4. Do you agree with the assertion that older is better? Why or why not? Is there a story or experience that leads you to hold this opinion strongly?

GETTING INTO YOUR YOUTH PASTOR'S HEAD

Chapter Thirteen

THE ART OF UNEARTHING ASSUMPTIONS

The senior pastor-youth pastor relationship is extremely important to the health of your ministry. Unfortunately, misunderstandings are common between youth pastors and senior pastors. The two have a tendency to misread each other. Needless to say, the relationship demands a certain amount of work to maintain.

With that in mind, let's try a short exercise.

Take a guess.
What do you think this is?

Before you turn the page, come up with your guess.

Okay, now that you've guessed, look at this image.
Do you want to change your answer?

Now what do you think?
Did you guess well?

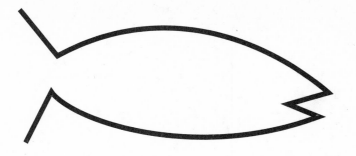

Did you guess a fish? Was that your original answer?

When I've shown this image to folks over the years, I've heard a lot of different guesses, including an eye, the top of a soda can (specifically Mountain Dew), an Egyptian hieroglyphic, and the car from *The Flintstones.*

When you guessed what the picture was, you made an inference. You weren't certain what the image would be, but you took an educated guess. If you didn't guess, then you inferred that taking a guess wasn't really necessary. Either way, you read between the lines. You filled in the blanks. That's essentially what it means to infer.

People have a knack for filling in the blanks with familiar information. It's a natural thing to do. You fill in the blanks when you have a conversation, watch the news, take an interest in a politician, listen to a sermon, get advice from a friend, or have a discussion with a staff member.

You infer while you're reading this book that you understand what I'm saying. You might skip entire sections because you look at the title or read a few sentences and convince yourself that you know where I'm going with it. As you read, you use your past experiences to make assumptions about me, and what I'm about.

People do the same thing to you, too. As a church leader, people associate you with certain things, certain beliefs, and certain attitudes. Their inferences may or may not be correct.

Let's look at inference in action: You preach a sermon on the unconditional love of God. You speak for 35 minutes, using story after story and making point after point. Everything you say reinforces the message you're hoping to drive home: God loves people unconditionally.

After the service, you overhear a conversation in the lobby. A man is telling his friend how happy he is that the church is going to embrace technology in new ways and how thrilled he is that you preached about it from the pulpit. You're confused. Your mind quickly reflects on what you said. You did give an illustration on how God can use technology, specifically a text message on your cell phone, to show his love to someone. The illustration was 120 seconds long. But the guy in the lobby thought it was your main point. You get frustrated. How could that guy, who happens to be a computer-software developer, hear only that point of the sermon and nothing else?

Before you can straighten him out, a woman approaches you. She seems upset. She says she's frustrated that you'd preach a sermon devaluing children. You recognize her as a mom of four kids in your church. Your head is spinning. What is she talking about? Devaluing children? You love kids. Your mind races. Later you listen to the tape of your sermon and hear yourself say, "Often people think about unconditional love when they think of their children, but we need to think about adults and their need for unconditional love as a church." You mentioned children in one sentence. That's it.

The man and woman in the latter illustration each made an inference about what you were trying to say. They jumped to conclusions. They filled in the blanks in ways you didn't intend.

The same phenomenon often occurs between a senior pastor and a youth pastor. Each takes what is said by the other and fills in the blanks. Each infers. Chris Argyris has developed a tool that's helpful in understanding how inference occurs. He calls it the ladder of inference.[3]

---

[3] The ladder of inference was developed by Chris Argyris. The material and concepts I'm showing here are adapted from Peter M. Senge, Art Kleiner, Charlotte Roberts, Richard B. Ross, and Bryan J. Smith, *The Fifth Discipline Fieldbook: Strategies and Tools for Building a Learning Organization* (New York, N.Y.: Doubleday Dell Publishing Group, Inc., 1994).

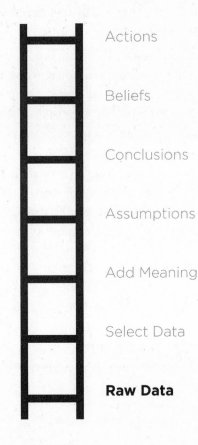

Actions

Beliefs

Conclusions

Assumptions

Add Meaning

Select Data

Raw Data

Raw Data

Life is happening all around you. So much is going on that you can't focus on it all. The hum of the air conditioner, a siren in the distance, a dozen voices talking in the room, the smell of coffee, the clang of a cup being dropped, the words of someone speaking to you, and the color of everything in the room are just some of the things vying for your attention. If you had a video camera, you might catch more of the Raw Data of life. But all you have are your senses. So the first step on the ladder of inference is to acknowledge that no matter how hard you try, you can't take everything in. You must select some data from the whole.

Actions

Beliefs

Conclusions

Assumptions

Add Meaning

Select Data

Raw Data

Select Data

Remember the inferences of the computer-software developer and the mom of four? Out of all the Raw Data in your sermon, they chose to focus on two extremely specific points. Everyone selects data—every day, all the time. There's simply more life and information than you can take in, so you select information from Raw Data.

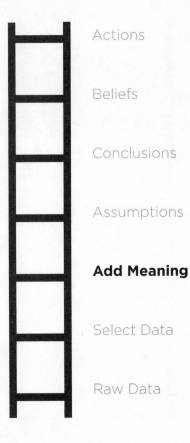

Actions

Beliefs

Conclusions

Assumptions

Add Meaning

Select Data

Raw Data

Add Meaning

What happens next is that people bring their personal experience to bear on the data they select. They ask questions such as, "Is this good or bad?" and "Does it have value?"

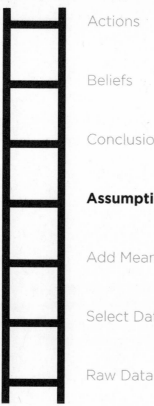

Actions

Beliefs

Conclusions

Assumptions

Add Meaning

Select Data

Raw Data

Make Assumptions

This step represents a big leap in reasoning. To make assumptions, people give themselves suggestions as to what's happening based on the selected data and the meaning they added.

Actions

Beliefs

Conclusions

Assumptions

Add Meaning

Select Data

Raw Data

Draw Conclusions
This is where people land after they make a leap in reasoning.

Actions

Beliefs

Conclusions

Assumptions

Add Meaning

Select Data

Raw Data

Establish Beliefs

In this step, people decide what they believe about others and about ideas, concepts, and philosophies.

Actions

Beliefs

Conclusions

Assumptions

Add Meaning

Select Data

Raw Data

Take Action
When people believe something, it informs and influences their actions.

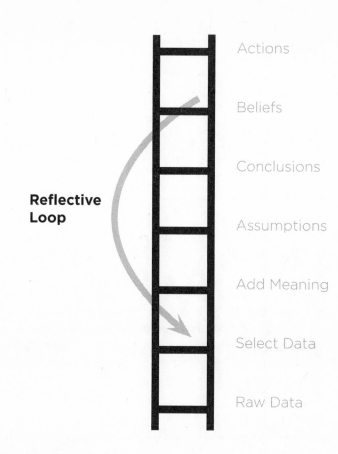

Reflective Loop

- Actions
- Beliefs
- Conclusions
- Assumptions
- Add Meaning
- Select Data
- Raw Data

Reflective Loop

The things people believe today will influence the information they select tomorrow. This "loop effect" causes beliefs to be reinforced each time data is selected.

That's why change is so hard for some people in your church. Their experience tells them how things should be done, and it's been reinforced by every example they've selected from the past.

To change action and behavior in a church means to break the beliefs and conclusions people have about what church should look like. Don't you love it? This stuff makes me giddy.

Here are some practical examples of how we make assumptions and climb the ladder of inference.

MARK RIDDLE AND FRIED CHICKEN

Start at the bottom of the inference ladder and work your way up through the following true story.

This is an odd but true story. I went 15 years without eating fried chicken. There was a time during those 15 years when I realized it was probably the flu or a virus that had made me sick, and not the chicken. But even after I understood chicken was okay for me to eat, I still avoided it. Not eating chicken had become part of who I was, and it was a hard habit to break.

Reflective Loop
A few months later, my buddy got sick and missed a few days of school. When he returned, I asked if he'd eaten chicken. He had—
two days before he fell ill. This confirmed my belief that fried chicken is dangerous for some people to eat.

Action
I'm going to avoid eating fried chicken.

Belief
Fried chicken is dangerous for some people to eat—and not just in the cardiovascular sense.

Conclusion
I'm allergic to fried chicken.

Assumption
The fried chicken made me sick and caused me to puke.

Add Meaning
Being sick is bad and should be avoided, if possible.

Select Data
I woke up in the middle of the night, got sick, puked, and went home.

Raw Data
When I was eight years old, I spent the night at my cousin's house. We watched movies and ate homemade fried chicken for dinner.

A YOUTH PASTOR'S PERSPECTIVE

Here's another example of how inference affects us. Again, start at the bottom rung and read up.

Notice that the youth pastor in this example didn't know who was calling the senior pastor. He simply assumed the worst. We don't know why the senior pastor answered the phone. We can only infer. If it's a random call, then the youth pastor's assumption might have some merit. But if it's the daughter of the senior pastor who's home sick and alone, then it's completely appropriate for the senior pastor to have answered the phone.

In this scenario, both people make assumptions. The senior pastor assumes it's okay to answer the phone. The youth pastor assumes it's just a random phone call. In this case, the youth pastor should be able to pause on the ladder of inference to recognize that he doesn't have all the information he needs. He shouldn't allow himself to rush to judgment.

This kind of thinking takes work. Let's look at another example—this time from the perspective of the senior pastor.

Action
I'm going to stop trying to engage my senior pastor in my life and ministry.

Belief
My senior pastor would rather spend his time with other people and doesn't have time for youth ministry.

Conclusion
My senior pastor doesn't value me or the youth ministry, even though he says he does.

Assumption
My senior pastor believes everyone else is more important than the youth pastor.

Add Meaning
It's rude to answer the phone when you're in a scheduled meeting.

Select Data
He interrupted me to answer the phone and talk.

Raw Data
My senior pastor's phone rings during one of my few scheduled one-on-one meetings with him.

THE ART OF UNEARTHING ASSUMPTIONS

THE STAFF MEETING

Notice that we don't know why the youth pastor was late for the staff meeting. The senior pastor assumed the worst in the situation. Perhaps this was a power play by the youth pastor—a passive-aggressive move to show the senior pastor how he feels about his leadership. Or perhaps the youth pastor was involved in a car accident, and he'd been performing CPR for the last 30 minutes to keep a victim alive until the ambulance arrived. We really don't know. Chances are, the youth pastor has been late before, but we still don't really know why.

The way to unearth assumptions is to develop the discipline of not climbing the ladder—and withholding judgment—until more information is gained.

Action
I'm not going to trust the youth pastor with anything important.

Belief
We can't count on the youth pastor. He's unreliable.

Conclusion
The youth pastor always comes in late.

Assumption
He deliberately came in late.

Add Meaning
Time is valuable, and the youth pastor knew when the meeting was supposed to start.

Select Data
The youth pastor showed up at 9:30 a.m.

Raw Data
The staff meeting was scheduled for 9 a.m.

LESSONS FROM THE LADDER OF INFERENCE

We climb the ladder of inference many times every day, in many different situations. The new data we select in those situations is influenced by what we believe. That means we're likely to see things that reinforce what we already believe—or what we spend our time thinking about.

Consider the man and woman in the church lobby after the sermon on God's unconditional love. Certain data from the sermon triggered their radars because they already had well-founded beliefs in those areas. Unfortunately, those well-founded beliefs kept them from hearing what the sermon was actually trying to say.

Sometimes what we believe to be the truth is actually only part of the truth. That's because of our tendency to deal with only a small part of the data we receive, and not all of it. Our response to this fact should be humility. Since we don't have all of the information, it's difficult to be dogmatic about our opinion of how things should be. This makes listening important.

We must develop a discipline of withholding judgment in conversations until we have sufficient information. We must ask questions instead of jumping to conclusions so we make informed decisions regarding ministry and relationships. That means we must initially be advocates for the people speaking to us and see ourselves as on the same team, even when the information we hold tells us otherwise.

There is wisdom in constantly and consistently asking yourself hard questions regarding what you believe about people, volunteers, staff, personalities, programs, and ministry, because we all have a tendency to believe things that simply aren't true. An unwillingness to engage in self-examination will result in an inability to change, a stale faith, and a narrow view of ministry—all of which will negatively impact your effectiveness as a leader.

Your staff, including your youth pastor, needs to understand how the ladder of inference works so that you can develop a culture of listening, advocacy, and inquiry. We can overcome wrong assumptions by becoming more aware of our own thinking, finding ways to make our personal reasoning more evident, and learning about the thinking of others.

THE ART OF UNEARTHING ASSUMPTIONS

THE LADDER OF INFERENCE IN ACTION

I'd been consulting and coaching with a church for more than a year. Most of my time was spent with the senior pastor and the youth leadership team, which was composed of about five lay leaders. There was no official staff person for the youth ministry, so those five people did most of the work. In most churches, some of those folks would've been paid for the leadership and oversight they provided. It's good to have lay leadership willing to do that. But in this case, it led to a problem.

As the youth leadership team implemented their programs, they felt that the paid staff was getting in their way. First of all, the fact that all of the youth leadership team had full-time jobs prevented them from getting together with the church staff to communicate what they were doing. For instance, the volunteer responsible for administration, communication, and mail-outs (or someone on her team) would go into the youth office and work on the church's computer. Different team members would come in and input names into the mailing list. Others would come in and make copies. They would tell the staff who they were, but the staff didn't really understand.

This led to some significant misunderstandings between the youth leadership team and the church staff. The staff didn't really know who these people were and what gave them the authority to use the church office, computers, and equipment. The staff assumed they were random people using the church's resources for their random agendas. Even though there was a comprehensive plan and detailed organizational system, the staff didn't know about it. The volunteers experienced the confusion of the staff as a hindrance to the youth ministry. They started to say things like, "The staff doesn't care about youth ministry," and "They're a bunch of control freaks."

I scheduled a Saturday morning meeting with the staff and the youth leadership team as soon as everyone's schedules allowed— which turned out to be five weeks later. With that kind of delay before a face-to-face conversation between the two groups could happen, we needed to find a way to keep the situation from getting ugly in the meantime. Both teams were jumping to conclusions about the other.

I introduced the ladder of inference with the youth leadership team and helped them understand how they were climbing it regularly in their experiences with the church staff. Each week it seemed as though the youth leadership team had another story to tell of a staff person who was frustrating them. But to their credit, they began to withhold judgment.

Five weeks of incidents occurred, but the team refused to believe they had all the information about what was happening. All evidence seemed to point to the fact that the staff consisted of a bunch of control freaks. When the youth leadership team finally met with the staff, I explained everything in detail. Once the blanks were filled in, everyone understood one another better. The youth leadership team had better information. They realized the church staff wasn't against them. In fact, the staff was very much for them.

We never really know all the facts about any situation. So any time we're tempted to make a judgment, we must recognize that there's information we don't have that would better inform our decisions.

ASSUMPTIONS ABOUT YOUTH PASTORS

Your youth pastor needs you to reflect on your assumptions about youth ministry. Your entire staff must be committed to unearthing assumptions about one another and one another's ideas. For example, when you think of the term *youth pastor*, how many of the following stereotypes come to mind?

- Must be very young (19-25) because old youth pastors (people over 25) can't connect with kids.

- Must be super energetic and hip. Can't be a nerd, geek, dork, or uncool in any way.

- Doesn't like theology.

- Loves to think about music, movies, and pop culture.

- Has a preoccupation with chocolate pudding and includes it in youth ministry activities whenever possible.

- Creates chaos.

- A maverick.

- Only relates to kids (people under 18).

- Doesn't work well with parents.

- Lives an unbalanced schedule. Youth ministry is his life.

- Must be good looking.

- Must be male.

- Musical enough to lead worship.

- Just a big kid who can't be taken seriously.

- A lone ranger; not a team player.

- Just likes to goof off. For him, youth ministry is just a big play-ground.

- One day aspires to be a senior pastor.

Some people in your congregation will always believe one or more of these stereotypes. But this list highlights exactly the sort of issues that are best resolved before you hire a youth pastor.

THE CONSEQUENCES OF FAULTY ASSUMPTIONS

1. Isolation.

This happens when communication breaks down and assumptions are made. Office arrangements in the average church contribute to this *isolation*. The youth pastor's office is usually located near the gym or youth room—isolated from the other staff offices.

Signs of isolation may be subtle—a person who used to be vocal in staff meetings no longer speaking up, for example. The person's isolation may have been caused by a misunderstanding or feelings of being undervalued. Isolation is fertile ground for further misunderstandings. Remember the reflective loop from the ladder of inference? Isolation creates tension. When you feel tension with a staff person, it's imperative that you address it as soon possible. Isolation is the first step down the road that leads to a youth pastor's resignation. Work relentlessly at maintaining healthy relationships with people in your church.

2. Alienation.

While isolation is relationally *neutral*, alienation is relationally *negative*. Isolated staff members feel alone. Alienated staff members build cases against people they see as problems. The good news is that some staff members can pull themselves out of their feelings of alienation. They can be reconnected with the staff members they took issue with. Working through the ladder of inference and unearthing wrong assumptions can help. In other words, alienation can be temporary—but not without intervention or someone's breaking the pattern of wrong thinking and assumptions that led to the sense of isolation.

3. Condemnation.

Staff members who feel isolated, then alienated, often move to condemnation. Generally speaking, condemnation is the point of no return. Condemning another staff person is semipermanent and usually signals that the end is near.

Alienation and isolation are more common among staff members than you might think. As I mentioned earlier in the book, a very high percentage of paid youth pastors said they would not attend the church they work for if they weren't paid to do so. These youth pastors have a strong loyalty to their students and their callings, but not necessarily to the senior pastors or the congregations.

Youth pastors commonly will keep their heads down and stick to doing ministry in their department until the situation becomes too unbearable for them to stay. They tell themselves, "I'm just here to do youth ministry. I'll ignore the dysfunction of the staff, the board, and the church." That's not a healthy solution.

Don't confuse the busyness of your youth pastor with isolation. Certainly busyness can lead to isolation, and you as the senior pastor can reach out to your youth pastor to reconnect and encourage her during those busy times.

The ladder of inference is a powerful tool to help us with our thinking. It can help us pause and reengage when we start to draw conclusions about our staffs. Isolation, alienation, and condemnation are rampant within senior pastor-youth pastor relationships and are a direct result of relational neglect. Though youth pastors may have reputations for being lone rangers, most desire to be mentored by their supervisors.

DISCUSSION QUESTIONS FOR YOU AND YOUR STAFF

1. What stands out most to you in this chapter?

2. Has there ever been a time when our staff climbed the ladder of inference and drew a faulty conclusion? If so, when?

3. What are ways we can encourage better communication between us?

4. Can we give each other permission to ask questions when we feel like we're jumping to conclusions about another staff person? Can we do it even when it feels uncomfortable?

5. Are there stereotypes we hold about one another's roles that we need to expose and seek forgiveness for?

Chapter Fourteen

IF YOU AREN'T GOING TO MENTOR YOUR YOUTH PASTOR, YOU DON'T DESERVE ONE

I wish my pastor knew how much respect and love I have for him in his continual support, encouragement, and love for the student ministry at our church.

—JEFF

I wish my senior pastor would have been totally honest and up front with me from the get-go. Taken some time to get to know me as a person. To support me. To offer me a little care. Truth was, I would have done anything he asked. I was just dying for leadership.

—BRIAN

When someone in our congregation dies, [my senior pastor] takes me with him [to visit the family] because he knows I need to know how to do it. He helped find ways for us to connect—and not always about ministry. Every day, even if it was just a moment or two, we'd talk about something that wasn't ministry related. He'd let me get into trouble and not bail me out, unless it was really going to hurt me. [He] let me preach, lead worship, and would take me to committee meetings, even though I didn't want to go at first. By attending the committee meetings, he taught me, a green youth pastor, about how the church works and about people's tendencies, which is benefiting me now years later. I loved it when he was my pastor.

—JAY

Kevin had been on staff for about a year, and the ministry was growing quickly. Kevin's reviews from his supervisor indicated that he was exceeding expectations for ministry growth, volunteer recruitment, and program development. But something else was going on under the surface. Kevin was really struggling with personal issues. He was trying to figure out how to maintain a personal walk with God, be a solid husband, and do a good job in vocational ministry. The ministry environment was energizing, but Kevin's wife was struggling, and Kevin's connection with God seemed to be increasingly integrated into his job. Not only was he becoming a "professional Christian," his schedule made it increasingly difficult to maintain friendships with people his own age.

Kevin knew he was in desperate need of mentoring from his senior pastor, Steve. In one of his regular meetings with Steve, Kevin brought up his personal struggles.

"Steve, I need some help with something. I need to be mentored by you or Kyle [the associate pastor] or someone. I'm really struggling to find some balance between my life and ministry."

Steve replied, "You'll have to look somewhere else for that. The church staff is here for the congregation. We hire staff because we think they can handle it and take care of themselves. What sense would it make, Kevin, to hire someone who's going to take our time to mentor? We would never do that."

Kevin was shocked. The next few minutes were a blur. He said something about the uniqueness of vocational ministry and needing input from someone in the trenches. But Steve's answer was clear. If you want to be mentored, it's not going to be by the pastoral staff of this church.

My friend Scott—a youth ministry veteran who provides oversight to youth ministry staff—says this about the temptation to not mentor a youth pastor:

We [senior pastors and executive pastors] struggle because we're looking for the ideal, for a youth pastor who doesn't need to be pastored. It's like the 22-year-old guy who's looking for a wife who doesn't need a lot of attention. "Do I really need to tell her I love her, do the flowers, and the dates, and the dishes? Can't I just come home and eat dinner and make love when I want to?"

"Can't I just find a youth pastor who does a great job and doesn't need a lot of coddling?"

All pastors need to be nurtured. They need to be pastored. Especially if the trend is to hire 21- to 30-year-olds. These are incredibly formative years in a young man or woman's life. They are more prone to feel confident in their decision-making, but they don't have any wisdom for their decision-making, so they're going to make bad decisions regularly, and they're going to feel confident about them. So they need older people to help temper that. It's all about relationships.

If you're simply hiring an individual to perform a list of tasks in the youth department, you're doing a disservice to your church, yourself, the parents, and the youth of your church. Remember, in the church, hiring is never simply about doing a job.

Sadly, it's becoming normal for churches to hire youth pastors and not give them the care they desire and need. Over the last few years, I've spoken with hundreds of youth pastors who've told me their stories. Many had left ministry altogether, unable to make sense of the calling they received from God—and the isolation and painful experiences they lived through being on a church staff. The disconnection they felt often related directly to their relationships with their senior pastors or some other significant church leader.

Church leaders have found that this kind of leadership style not only doesn't work, it's also a subtle form of manipulation and abuse because it dehumanizes and alienates the staff person.

For senior pastors, it's a matter of stewardship. Youth pastors are a tremendous resource for God and God's kingdom. Pastors who fail to mentor their staff are squandering the lives God has shaped for a great future in ministry.

In some cases, a senior pastor mentoring a youth pastor is simply not a viable solution. In those situations, the senior pastors and youth pastors need to ensure two things:

1. That a viable relationship is still in place between them.

2. That the youth pastor is mentored by someone on staff—someone she trusts who carries significant authority with the senior pastor. A random relationship with a church member can be a wonderful way to grow, but the mentor must have authority within the church to give her the kind of mentoring she needs.

MENTORING IS NOT CONTROLLING OR MICROMANAGEMENT

When I started at [the church], the senior pastor called me into his office on Thursday before my first Sunday night of youth group. He asked me to bring in a report with what I'd scheduled for the night. I'd been in youth ministry for eight years and never had this happen before. My pastor looked over my report and then said, "This game's not going to work, and I don't like this song, so you'll *need* to find a new game and a new song for these slots." I didn't know what to say. It's been that way for six months. I would never have come to this church if I had known it would be like this. I'm miserable. The kids are great, but my pastor is too controlling. I'm going to get out the first chance I get.

—KENT (SALESMAN AND FORMER YOUTH PASTOR)

Let's be honest for a minute. There are some controlling people out there. I've written this book for folks who aren't micromanagers, so chances are, if you've made it this far, this section isn't for you. However, I feel the need to include it. For micromanagers, being a part of every decision is critical to their leadership style. If you're a senior pastor and find yourself micromanaging your youth pastor, you'll likely find that you don't keep that youth pastor very long. Micromanaging makes your youth pastors feel that you don't trust them. They feel this way because you *don't* trust them.

Micromanaging is abuse of power. It is the pursuit of ego in the name of "excellence," often to the extent that the controlling individual himself is fooled into believing this.

Here are some signs that you might be micromanaging:

1. You want to give input into the details of each weekly program.

2. You often feel the need to correct your youth pastor's behavior by constantly developing new rules.

3. You've lost trust in your youth pastor.

4. Your youth pastor often uses phrases such as:

    -   "I want to do youth ministry how you want, but I don't know what your vision is for the youth ministry."

    -   "How do you feel the youth ministry is going?"

    -   "I feel like you don't trust me."

Do you recognize yourself in any of these signs? If so, it may be time to reevaluate your management style.

DISCUSSION QUESTIONS FOR YOU AND YOUR STAFF

1. (To the youth pastor) Do you know anyone who's had an experience like Kevin's? If so, what happened?

2. (To the senior pastor) What do you think about the quote from Steve, Kevin's senior pastor: "What sense would it make, Kevin, to hire someone who's going to take our time to mentor? We would never do that"?

3. Why do you think so many youth pastors end up leaving ministry? Can you give an example of someone you know who represents this perspective?

4. How do you feel about youth pastor turnover? What can we do to deal with the system that causes it?

5. What is your opinion of the statement, "If you aren't going to mentor your youth pastor, you don't deserve one"? Explain.

6. (To the youth pastor) Have you ever felt as though you were being controlled or micromanaged? If so, when? How would you describe the difference between mentoring and controlling micromanagement?

Chapter Fifteen

THE HUMANITY OF IT ALL

I wish pastors knew that it is never okay to tell the youth minister, "I'm your boss. I'm not your friend."

—DAVID

Dave, a youth pastor, was dealing with some major issues in his life. Chris, his senior pastor, sat down to talk, at Dave's request. What Chris heard startled him. Dave was in a dark place, struggling with depression and other tough issues. After Dave spoke for a bit, Chris interrupted. "I want you to know something I think is important for you to understand." Chris looked Dave in the eyes. "You are more important to me than the work you do here."

A year later Dave told me how those few simple words had impacted him deeply. "You are more important to me than the work you do here." Those are words youth pastors long to hear. In a time when many churches operate like machines that build momentum—at the expense of the souls of their staff members—Chris showed he valued Dave as a person.

I'm going to let you in on a little secret: A growing number of youth pastors believe that their senior pastors value their production more than they value them as people. In these churches, the bottom line is more important than the people who make the bottom line possible. Maybe this shocks you. But it's increasingly more common in churches that consider themselves progressive.

As more and more churches look to the business world for management models, people start to become expendable, and the end starts to justify the means. Words such as *excellence, momentum, goals, deliverables,* and *measurable results* have infiltrated the church world over the last 35 years as churches look to more capitalistic styles of leadership.

Youth pastors and other staff members have felt the brunt of this shift. They've seen firsthand the declining value church leaders place on their staff.

The trend isn't restricted to the church, either. In the last week, I heard the following quotes:

- A parent to her child: "You got such great grades this semester! That's why I love you, Sweetie!"

- A coach to his quarterback: "You are worthless. You keep overthrowing the receiver."

- A businessman to a homeless man: "Get a job, you piece of @#$&."

- A teacher to a student: "You will never amount to anything."

If you had a few moments with each person quoted, what would you say? Maybe something like, "People aren't valuable because of what they produce—not in God's economy, at least. They're valuable because of who they are."

Having a staff person work for you means you have a responsibility to care for and nurture that person's soul. You have to value the *whole* person. Part of that valuing process is exercising wisdom in what you ask the staff member to do. You need to challenge your youth pastor to be all that God created her to be. And you need to give her attainable expectations.

In order to do that, you have to know her well enough to know what she can and can't accomplish. Asking someone to do something she can't do is unhealthy, to say the least.

TRUE VALUE

A youth pastor can do a great job, create great programs, and have great relationships with kids, parents, and staff—and still feel unvalued. Many youth pastors will walk through walls for their senior pastors, whether they feel supported or not. But you won't keep great youth pastors if they feel like you only care about their performance. Great youth pastors believe that the way the church staff functions and treats one another is a microcosm of the entire church.

Church leaders are living examples of God's unique economy. Consider it mission work in an American society that sees people as cogs in a wheel to cross a finish line. This is the tension that today's pastors must deal with. They must try to coax maximum performance from their staff while at the same time reassuring staff of their value apart from their performance.

Bottom line: Youth pastors need to be loved and valued as people more than for what they produce as staff members. That doesn't mean you shouldn't have expectations for them or not hold them accountable for doing the job you expect them to do. Most youth pastors want to do a great job and are willing to make great sacrifices for your church and the kingdom. The balance is relational. If you have a good relationship with your youth pastor, you can challenge him in profound ways, and he'll respect you because he knows you trust and value him. Outside of a relationship, people feel like part of a machine.

Believe it or not, there's a growing trend among business executives with their MBAs to go to seminary to learn this very principle. It's interesting to me that smart business people are starting to understand that valuing people in the workplace actually increases quality and productivity, while the church seems to be learning the opposite lesson.

I first learned about this trend in a March 2005 article in *Fast Company* magazine titled, "God and Mammon at Harvard." The article offered examples of business leaders learning to value relationships and people over the bottom line by taking classes at Harvard

Divinity School. Take Tom Chappell, CEO of the natural toothpaste company Tom's of Maine.

In Chappell's case, the experience was transformative. He had come to the divinity school at age 43, after an aggressive growth period in his company that had left him emotionally and spiritually drained. The business was thriving, but he was finding more emptiness than fulfillment in success, he says. Many entrepreneurs would argue that when you reach that point, it's time to flip the business, buy a sailboat, and travel the world. But Chappell was haunted by a comment from his pastor's wife: "What makes you think Tom's of Maine isn't your ministry?" she asked.

So Chappell struck a deal with his board. He'd spend half a week in Cambridge, Massachusetts, as a student, and half a week in Kennebunk, Maine, as CEO. "I got down there, and the business did very well," he says, "so everyone suggested I stay and do a little more praying." Four years later, degree in hand, he invited his HDS mentor, Richard Niebuhr, to meet with his board and executive team to begin mapping out the company's new direction. That included drafting a new mission statement that drew from 18th-century New England theologian Jonathan Edwards's belief that the nature of being is relational rather than individual. So Tom's of Maine pledged to honor its moral obligations to all its stakeholders—employees, owners, suppliers, consumers, community, and the environment."[4]

Business is changing to value people more. This is an area in which the church can teach and lead business—if it learns to do this well.

[4] Linda Tischler, "God and Mammon at Harvard," *Fast Company* 94 (May 2005): 80.

Years ago, a major Christian record label (Sparrow) hired me to spend five weeks as the road pastor for five teens who'd formed a group. The group was popular with Disney and was touring with another major artist and group who were not Christians, meaning it would be a very different tour environment than any of the teenagers had experienced to that point. My instructions were clear: I wasn't being hired to be a chaperone, a road manager, or a tutor. I was hired to be a pastoral presence on the road for those five kids.

As I interviewed with the president of Sparrow, Peter York, I asked him a direct question: "What if we are on the road, and the kids have four more shows, but they are emotionally, spiritually, or otherwise burned-out—and it's my opinion that they need to cancel the shows and come home? What would you do?"

Peter's response changed my opinion of the Christian music industry for the better. He said, "Our policy is to do what is right for our artist. Doing the right thing for them is always the best thing for our company."

Local church translation: *Doing the right thing for your youth pastor is always the right thing for your youth ministry. Doing the right thing for your staff is always the right thing for your church.*

Your youth pastor has a deep desire to be understood and valued by you. Make it a point to consistently affirm her as a person. Pray for her. Listen to her stories and struggles. Keep an open door for her. Talk to her about things other than work and ministry.

DISCUSSION QUESTIONS FOR YOU AND YOUR STAFF

1. What do you think of the statement, "Value your youth pastor as a person more than what your youth pastor produces as a staff member"?

2. Does it surprise you that so many youth pastors feel undervalued?

3. Do you, as the senior pastor, ever feel as though you're valued only for what you produce?

4. What are ways we as a staff neglect to value our volunteers as people?

Chapter Sixteen

ESCAPING THE CONSTANT EMOTIONAL BURN OF MINISTRY

My pastor doesn't even answer his cell phone on Friday and Saturday because those are his days off. Some people complain about it, but that is how he keeps himself fresh. I really respect that. It made it easier for me to take care of my family, too.

—JOY

I wish he knew how glad I am to have him as a pastor. I wish he knew how many more days he should take off, and how to let so many of the complaints roll off his back.

—TODD

Our society is not a community radiant with the love of Christ, but a dangerous network of domination and manipulation in which we can easily get entangled and lose our soul. The basic question is whether we ministers of Jesus Christ have not already been so deeply molded by the seductive power of our dark world that we have become blind to our own and other people's fatal state and have lost the power and motivation to swim for our lives.

Just look for a moment at our daily routine. In general we are very busy people. We have meetings to attend, many visits to make, many services to lead. Our calendars are filled with appointments, our days and weeks filled with engagements, and our years filled with plans and projects. There is seldom a period in which we do not know what to do, and we move through life in such a distracted way that we do not even take the time and rest to wonder if any of the things we think, say, or do are worth thinking, saying, or doing.[5]

—HENRI J. M. NOUWEN

[5] Henri J. M. Nouwen, *The Way of the Heart: Desert Spirituality and Contemporary Ministry* (New York, N.Y.: HarperCollins, 1991).

A few years ago I sat down for an hour with Rick and Cathy. Rick was a part-time youth pastor who wanted input on his weekly four-hour Friday night program called "The Mountain" and how it fit within all his other programs at the church.

Rick did most of the talking while Cathy remained quiet. Rick had been a part-time youth pastor for almost a year at that point. His primary income for supporting his family of five came from his job as a self-employed plumber. I asked Rick how many hours a week he was spending doing youth ministry. His response was, "Twenty to twenty-five hours a week."

It didn't seem right. It didn't add up to me. Cathy seemed upset but remained quiet. So I asked her how many hours a week she thought he worked at the church. She said, "He's paid for 20 hours a week, but he works 50 to 60 hours a week, and it's affecting his plumbing business. He's only doing plumbing about 15 to 20 hours a week now, and we are really struggling."

Rick looked a bit embarrassed but then talked about how much he loved youth ministry and how he felt called to be spending that much time doing it. When I asked him how his senior pastor felt about him working so much, Rick's response surprised me. "Yeah, we've talked. He thinks it's great that I'm working that much. We get along well. It's fun getting together, coming up with new programs and ideas for youth ministry."

As I write this, I'm giving Rick and Cathy's senior pastor the benefit of the doubt. I'm going to assume that Rick was masterfully misleading the pastor as to how many hours he was really working and how many volunteers he had leading the program. I'm going to assume the best about the senior pastor—but it's difficult to do. You see, I knew something significant and life-altering was wrong within the first 15 minutes of my conversation with Rick and Cathy. Yet their senior pastor apparently hadn't recognized the problem.

I must confess that as I write this, years later, I'm still feeling the pain of what was shared in those moments. It's an intentional decision on my part not to assume that the senior pastor was ignoring the pain in order to gain a little momentum in his church's youth ministry. Rick was really hurting his family. Before the end of the conversation,

Cathy was sobbing because, for the first time in a year, someone else recognized her pain and her family's predicament. Someone else recognized the burden she was bearing and the upheaval the situation was causing.

This is what I, a stranger, told Rick: "Look at Cathy. You are hurting your wife by working so many hours at the church and by not working enough plumbing jobs to pay your bills. You may be right. You may be called into youth ministry. I can see your passion for connecting to kids. But *this* is not the way to go about it. You've only been doing this for a year, and your family is deeply wounded. You can't keep doing this. Do you hear me? It can't continue. You must make big changes right now to save your marriage. Your family are the most significant people you minister to. If it means you need to make "The Mountain" a monthly program instead of a weekly program, or quit leading it altogether, you need to do it. I want to see you in ministry for the long haul, but you'll never make it."

In other words, I told Rick what his senior pastor should have told him. I don't know if Rick heard me. My interaction with him and Cathy lasted all of 55 minutes.

Just so we're clear: It wasn't the senior pastor's fault that Rick was hurting his marriage. It was not the senior pastor's fault that Rick had issues that drove him to such behavior. It wasn't the senior pastor's fault that Rick was mishandling his work schedule. But the senior pastor should have seen those things and intervened. The senior pastor should have known because the senior pastor should have been involved.

Maybe there were unique circumstances in Rick's situation. I've seen them before. But they're hard to imagine. The cold, hard truth is that sometimes leaders are tempted to believe that the benefits of having a part-time youth pastor working 50 to 60 hours a week outweigh the toll it takes on the youth pastor's family. In the quest for a great youth ministry—one that helps a lot of kids—sometimes church leaders are willing to gamble on the youth pastor's family.

Your youth pastor needs you, as senior pastor, to help her make healthy choices about the amount of time she invests in her ministry.

She needs you to hold her accountable for taking days off and working reasonably healthy hours.

WHAT VACATION IS—AND ISN'T

Toward that end, you and your church need to recognize that youth camps, mission trips, youth ministry conferences, and retreats are workdays for your youth pastor. The tendency of some churches to call them vacation days is ludicrous—an idea that stems from ignorance of what goes on in those places.

Treating them as vacation days is an exploitation of your staff's good will. Those experiences are not only work related, but also physically and emotionally draining on your staff. Vacations are breaks from *work*—as in, without kids and without a ministry focus.

OFFICE HOURS

It's naive to believe that meaningful youth ministry takes place exclusively in the church building. And it's a mistake to believe that a youth pastor should spend most of her time in her office. Regular hours aren't a bad idea so that the other staff members know how to get in touch with the youth pastor, but in our technological age, no one is out of reach.

Case in point: I'm writing this in a local coffee shop. My wife just called me on Skype (a free program) from our home, and I had a video chat with her to discuss our plans for later in the day. Then I blew kisses to my kids and went back to writing. A youth pastor keeping an eight-to-five, five-days-a-week schedule in an office is unreasonable for a healthy youth ministry.

Youth pastors need flexibility in their schedules. Todd, a friend of mine and a youth pastor, taught me about the block system of scheduling. Divide the day into three time blocks: Morning (8 a.m. to noon), afternoon (noon to 5 p.m.) and evening (5 p.m. to 10 p.m.). Expect your youth pastor to work two of those time blocks every workday.

LEADING BY EXAMPLE

Part of the role of a pastor is to live life in a healthy rhythm with God. Busyness and a hurried schedule may be the norm for your congregation, but you and your staff should try to set an example of healthy living. I'm not just talking about physical health, diet, and exercise, but also the way you spend your time. Get over your messiah-complex-veiled-in-workaholism and relax a little. It's good for you.

In the process, you may help your youth pastor do the same. Your staff is watching you to learn how to pastor the people in your church. Many will follow your example, for better or worse. The way you live and the way you work set the norm for your staff.

I was teaching a seminary course on youth ministry. Two of the people taking the course were Craig, a youth pastor, and Jim, a senior pastor, from a local church. Jim was taking the course with his youth pastor to learn with him and build their relationship. Over the course of the class, we would often pause and ask Jim about his experience and perspective as a senior pastor. One day we asked him what makes ministry so difficult. I remember his response:

"I've worked in business for years, and now I work in the church. Both are demanding jobs. Both can be very hard. But the hardest part of ministry is the emotional energy that it constantly demands. That's what makes ministry so difficult."

In business, you can leave at 5 p.m. and be done for the day. In ministry, even if you don't work another minute that evening, it's not uncommon for the emotional strain of the day to continue to weigh on you. There's a constant emotional burn in pastoral ministry that few understand. My friend Fr. Rob Merola reflected on this issue recently on his blog:

> One of the jobs I remember fondly is building a railroad tie wall. That was back when we were young and strong and invincible, meaning we could throw a tie over each shoulder, carry them to the desired location, hoist them in place, and swing a heavy sledge all day. It was good, honest work, and at the end of the day we felt like we had accomplished something.

Tired as we were, though, we'd go home, shower, and get a bite to eat, and then be ready to go back out for the evening.

I thought about that last Sunday afternoon when I think I was the most exhausted I have ever been in my life. I went home after church services and took a nap that lasted all afternoon. I did get up for an evening meeting at church, but basically went home right afterward and fell back asleep again. I was sitting in a chair and just couldn't keep my eyes open, couldn't even move a muscle (at least that is how it felt). At about 1 a.m. Linda woke me to ask me if I was coming to bed. Somehow I managed to stumble from the chair to the bed, where I went straight back to sleep in my clothes and on top of the sheets and didn't move until morning.

So why was I so exhausted? I think the output of emotional energy is even more draining than the output of physical energy. Yes, using one's body is demanding, but using one's heart is even more so. On Sunday afternoon our [missions] trip to Belize was over, our Vacation Bible School was over, and church services were over. All of them were great, but all of them required a great investment of heart and mind and soul. It wasn't until that moment that I could really let down.

But maybe there was another component, too. Administering communion that morning, I came to my oldest daughter and realized I would only do this on a regular basis one more Sunday. It is as strange for me to think of Christine leaving my church family as it is for me to think of her leaving our home. As you'd expect of a priest, her spiritual life and development mean everything to me. Now the time is coming when I need to entrust that to someone else...[6]

Living with that constant emotional burn can be managed by regular time away from work, by finding a hobby you enjoy, by developing a discipline of playfulness, and by remembering that ministry is a long journey. Time away from the job isn't a luxury; it's a necessity. It's difficult for church boards to grasp the uniqueness of pastoral ministry. Thus, it can be difficult for them to empower their pastors to live in ways that are healthy.

In another blog post, Rob writes about a way he manages his identity and emotional health.

I'm 49 years old, with 50 not far on the horizon. These days I know that is still considered young, but it is old enough that at least some times I start to feel my age. One of the ways I know I am feeling my age is when I also feel the need to defy it.

I've also been a priest for 21 years; long enough that it is hard to remember what it was like not to be a priest. But I've never wanted to be a priest that was too "priestly"; I've never wanted to be so defined by my vocation that I forgot what it means to be an ordinary guy.

I think those are a couple of reasons I made my bonsai fishing trip. Part of it was just to see if I could. Could I drive 5 hours, fish 14 hours straight without even taking a break for food or water (and thus not need to take, uh, other breaks, if you get my drift), and then drive 5 more hours back home? Do I still have that physical capability?

The answer seems to be yes and no. I did it. But I also paid a price—I sure was sore the next day! There was no getting up and doing it all over again, which I may well have done were I a younger man.

Another part of it was simply to spend a day far differently than how I normally spend them. I fished all night long, when I would normally be sound asleep next to the warm and inviting body of my lovely wife. I waded streams and slogged through mud and scrabbled over rocks instead of sitting prim and proper at my desk. Instead of baptizing babies or distributing communion or writing a sermon, I caught fish. My whole world was reduced to a primal pursuit, elegant only in its simplicity, and in the freedom that comes from not having to be anything for anyone.

[6] Father Rob Merola is the rector of St. Matthew's Episcopal Church in Sterling, Virginia. Rob is a great writer, and I read his blog regularly. His address is daddyroblog.blogs.com.

Somewhere in there I found the assurance that Rob Merola, the little boy who before he was ever anyone else was just a kid who loved to cast a line into the water, is still alive and well.

I'm not sure I consider a bonsai fishing trip relaxing, but that's the way Rob maintains a healthy understanding of himself. Living a healthy rhythm gives you and your staff the ability to remember who you are, to feel alive, and to be whole.

One more thing: Every five to seven years, you and your youth pastor need to take a three-month sabbatical. Write a policy for the church and take it. Sabbatical is the historical practice of church leaders taking an extended break from their daily responsibilities. Most church leaders I visit with know what a sabbatical is and why it's important, yet few actually take sabbaticals. For some, it feels selfish to take three months off every seven years, so they simply don't ask for it. Others would take a sabbatical if there weren't so much to do.

Taking three months every seven years will provide perspective on life and ministry while nourishing your soul. I know that no one in your congregation gets to take that kind of time off, but none of them are pastors, either. You and your youth pastor will be better for taking sabbaticals. And so will your congregation.

DISCUSSION QUESTIONS FOR YOU AND YOUR STAFF

1. What stands out to you in Rick and Cathy's story? Why?

2. What are ways we can be more flexible with office hours and still stay connected?

3. What do you do for fun? When was the last time you did that?

4. On a scale of 1 to 10, with 1 being unhealthy and unbalanced and 10 being very healthy and balanced, how would you rate yourself personally?

5. What are ways we can help one another work in a healthy rhythm?

Chapter Seventeen

PASSION

Now I have a new senior pastor, and it's not going so well. We were reading a book together that caused us to dream a bit about what our church might look like in the future. We mapped it all out on a whiteboard. Then he said something I'll never forget. He said, "That seems like such a great shift, but why would we want to change to that kind of church? It sounds like a lot of work, and I'm going to retire in 10 years." That really affected me. You could hear my heart shattering. If that's what this church is going to be about, waiting for retirement, then I'm out.

—ARVELL

Kids need passion, not just for worship but for life.

—SOPHOMORE GUY

I feel awkward when I go to worship. I wonder, "Where's the life in this?" Sometimes I get into it.

—SIXTH-GRADE GIRL

When Christian Theology cannot embrace God's suffering love as its focal point—or worse, when it denies passion as the crux of Christian identity—the church has no basis on which to challenge the culture's claim on young people. Passionless Christianity has nothing to die for; it practices assimilation, not oddity. Passionless Christians lead sensible lives, not subversive ones; we are benignly "nice" instead of dangerously loving.[7]

—KENDA DEAN

[7] Kenda Creasy Dean, *Practicing Passion: Youth and the Quest for a Passionate Church* (Grand Rapids, Mich.: Eerdmans Publishing Co., 2004), 51-52.

Maybe it's because many youth pastors are young.

Maybe it's because youth pastors carry a lot of hope for the future.

Maybe it's because the youth pastors' constituency has a long life ahead of them in the church.

Maybe it's because youth pastors take the gospel seriously.

Whatever the reason, youth pastors want senior pastors to be passionate about ministry.

You won't keep a youth pastor if you don't lead and challenge her. Great youth pastors will not settle for *passionless* ministry or *passionless* leadership. They know that church staff members who are "mailing it in" can become barriers to the church's growth. They know that senior pastors who aren't willing to take risks harm the future of the church.

If you, as the senior pastor, are in a place where you're unwilling to make significant changes, then you need to inform your youth pastor candidates of that before you hire them. Most will appreciate your honesty. I don't mean to suggest that a senior pastor without passion for the gospel is a good thing. But I recognize that there are pastors who mail in their last few years in ministry for the pension. The best fit for a congregation like yours is a youth pastor who has similar feelings about change. If you already have a youth pastor on staff, you need to be open and honest about your reluctance to change so that she understands why it's difficult for you to support some of her ideas.

The heart of passion isn't emotional enthusiasm; it's sacrifice. It's born in the cross, and it's a call to radical, faithful living. Youth pastors want to make a difference in the kingdom and are willing to risk a lot to see it happen. Kids want to live for something worth dying for.

Too often the church inoculates teenagers and staff to this passion by expecting them to fall in line and "be nice." If that describes your church, you should consider it a success when teenagers leave your church after graduation. Churches will be held accountable for inoculating young people to the true power of the gospel and sending them into adulthood without faith.

Passionless churches teach students that Jesus is a supplement to accomplishing their own purposes in the world. Want to get into a good college? Add a little Jesus, be a good person, and presto! Need a spouse? That high-paying job? The way of Jesus becomes a moral boost to become all you want to be. Churches with such environments seek to make good citizens who don't rock the boat and are generally nice people.

The question regarding your church is this: Why would a high school student want to come? Is there an obvious reason a teenager would go out of his way to join your congregation? Duty isn't an acceptable answer.

To put it another way: How good is your good news?

Friends, gimmicks, events, pizza, and games are fun for a while. But kids are looking for good news—gospel truth. Will they find it in your church? Will they find it in your programs, people, structure, hope, and passion? Will they find a simplified and tamed gospel reduced to four spiritual laws? Or will they find a wild, dangerous, mysterious, expansive gospel that engages all of life?

Is the gospel still dangerous and immanent for you as a pastor? If the answer is yes, share your passion with your youth pastor and students. They need to see your passion, however you and your personality best exemplify it.

If the answer is no, you have a choice. You don't have to "mail it in" until you reach retirement age. Take a break or a sabbatical. Find someone you trust to talk to about it. Take action. Finish strong. Discover what it's like to rekindle the passion of God within you. The process of transformation in you may be what your church needs most.

DISCUSSION QUESTIONS FOR YOU AND YOUR STAFF

1. Passion is something of a relative concept. What does a passionate church look like to you?

2. How important is passion to you? Why?

3. How important is passion for your students? Why?

4. What does a passionate staff look like from your perspective?

5. In what ways do we show passion?

6. What are ways we could be a more passionate church? Staff?

7. Was there a time when you had more passion than you do now? If so, what happened?

Chapter Eighteen

TEAMWORK AND LOYALTY

I wish my senior pastor would understand that I have been called to youth ministry and nothing else. Youth ministry is a valid and worthwhile calling…just as valid and worthwhile as his.

—Brian

Kyle was hired to lead the high school ministry. Within his first few months on staff the senior pastor invited Kyle to participate in a design team for a new worship service aimed at connecting with high school students, their parents, and people under the age of 35. The senior pastor invited Kyle to join, telling him that his expertise would make the service work really well. Kyle had left a church where he served on a similar team, so it seemed natural for Kyle to contribute to the design of the new service in his new context.

The first few meetings were rocky. Kyle brought ideas to the table that he felt were creative and would work well, but none of them were being implemented. Instead the senior pastor came to the meeting with his ideas, seemed frustrated by Kyle's ideas, which he called distractions, and would assign Kyle various tasks at the end of the meeting. Kyle would suggest an idea and would express his willingness to lead the charge to complete the idea, but it always seemed to be shot down. Kyle was struggling and seriously contemplating stepping down from the service design team. He decided to share his frustrations with the senior pastor before he made any decisions.

He told the senior pastor something like this:

"When you invited me to be on the design team for this service, I was excited. I enjoy working with other staff and volunteers outside the youth ministry to connect with and serve our community. I was excited because I see the potential this service has in impacting our students as well. But right now I'm frustrated. I feel like my ideas aren't valued. I feel like I'm just being assigned a bunch of tasks that I don't think are all that great and fall way short of our best. I'm disappointed because I feel like I've been really trying, and I'm not sure if I've done something wrong that would cause you to disregard my ideas. It seems like you just want a team to implement your ideas rather than a team to actually design the service with you."

The response Kyle heard taught him a lot. It went something like this:

"Kyle, I'm glad you are on the team, but isn't this how the team at your previous church worked? I'm looking for someone to help me create a new service."

This was not the same kind of team Kyle had experienced previously, and as the conversation continued, it was clear there were two distinct understandings of what *team* actually meant. Kyle was looking for collaboration. He expected his ideas to receive equal weight to the other team members' ideas, and that together they would carry the weight and responsibility for this new service. The senior pastor wasn't looking for *collaboration*; he was looking for *cooperation*. In his mind he was responsible for the new service, therefore his ideas were more valuable than other team members' ideas. The senior pastor was looking for the team to cooperate with his ideas and implement them as he desired.

As this became clear to Kyle, he graciously stepped down from the design team. He has plenty of other responsibilities on his to-do list and isn't looking for more tasks to fill his day.

Collaboration and cooperation are both legitimate leadership styles for working with others. However, it's important that church leaders recognize which styles they prefer, and that you inform your youth pastors of those styles.

Though cooperation is at times imperative, youth pastors want to collaborate more than simply cooperate with a church leader's agenda for youth ministry and the church. It's safe to say that this can cause significant problems between a senior pastor and a youth pastor.

LOYALTY AND DISLOYALTY

What's often confusing for youth pastors is that these two distinct understandings for working together become an issue of loyalty. It's my observation that *loyalty* isn't a word youth pastors use very often, but it's a word I hear a lot from senior pastors. Youth pastors use the word *relationship* more than *loyalty*. From the perspective of a church leader who seeks cooperation above collaboration, a youth pastor who consistently gives input and suggestions will come across as arrogant or threatening, leaving the church leader to believe the youth pastor is not loyal. Neither party understands the other's perspective, and the youth pastor is left confused and wounded with his integrity questioned.

As a church leader it's important that you understand this isn't a loyalty issue. To mislabel it complicates the situation to a degree that's often irreparable.

Disloyalty is a common cause for senior pastors to lose trust in youth pastors and other staff. There are many forms in which this lack of loyalty (or perceived lack of loyalty) manifests itself.

1. The youth pastor engages in inappropriate conversations about the senior pastor or her ideas about things. These are situations in which the youth pastor actively lobbies for a different agenda to the other staff, volunteers, or students than the stated or expressed or assumed agenda of the senior pastor.

2. The youth pastor challenges the ideas of the senior pastor in a meeting. To a youth pastor, *team* means we all contribute

and express honest opinions about ideas. It's not a lack of loyalty to devalue an idea the senior pastor has in these kinds of settings, though many senior pastors confuse what the youth pastor is doing. It's not personal. In the mind of the youth pastor, he's acting in support and loyalty to the senior pastor by telling him this idea is a bad one, while to some senior pastors it feels like a personal attack or a display of disloyalty. Senior pastors who do this will always struggle to keep great youth pastors.

3. The youth pastor wants to collaborate, not simply cooperate, on the team.

Senior pastors feel threatened by the success of their youth pastors. But a great youth pastor will likely be better at some things than you are, just as you will be better at some things than your youth pastor is. This is especially true of older youth pastors. If the success of the youth pastor causes you to feel threatened, then it's not a loyalty issue; it's a personal issue. Don't hire arrogant people and don't be insecure when great staff members experience success.

Be careful with the *loyalty* word. Youth pastors, especially young youth pastors, do not give loyalty blindly, but they are actively seeking reasons to give you their loyalty, thus making it easy to earn—if you understand where they're coming from. Youth pastors desire to be loyal to God first, and loyalty to you is on down the list from there. Youth pastors assume loyalty as a part of a team. On a team, loyalty is given by all team members to one another. In other words, youth pastors assume they are loyal to you and that you are loyal to them.

You can't demand loyalty from a staff person. Demanding loyalty is a good way to lose it. Loyalty is earned by living with integrity and relentless faithfulness.

I've been hesitant to write so much about loyalty in this book. I've limited the topic to this chapter, and even it feels like I've written too much already. I'm uncomfortable writing about loyalty in the local church because there's often an unhealthy, codependent element to the loyalty conversation. While loyalty is an important quality, most

A NOTE TO THE YOUTH PASTOR

Never underestimate a senior pastor's desire and need for loyalty. If loyalty is a big, paramount issue for the senior pastor of the church you're candidating with, it may be best to look elsewhere.

people who obsess over it are controlling individuals who have tendencies toward emotional abuse. If you're looking for someone who will always do what you want, don't hire a youth pastor and buy a golden retriever instead. If you're afraid of the questions a youth pastor is asking, it's time for some personal self-examination.

DISCUSSION QUESTIONS FOR YOU AND YOUR STAFF

1. Is *loyalty* a word you as church leadership use very often?

2. Tell a story of when loyalty was an issue.

3. What was most helpful about the distinction between collaboration and cooperation?

4. Which fits your leadership style best?

5. Which fits you best when you serve on a team led by someone else?

Chapter Nineteen

I'VE GOT YOUR BACK!

When someone would come to complain about me or the youth ministry, my senior pastor would say, "Have you talked to Jay?" If they had not, he wouldn't listen to their comments on that subject anymore. He would deflect everything. He would never let anyone come to his office and gripe about me. He always pointed them toward me.

—JAY

I wish my current senior pastor knew how much his support means to me. I wish he knew how I appreciate the way he directs any complaints about me and my ministry to me instead of giving those with concerns a hearing.

—SHANNON

YOUR YOUTH PASTOR WANTS YOU TO HAVE HER BACK

This is a big deal.

When Jimmy was 21 and in his third year of youth ministry, he hired Eric, a junior in high school and a member of the youth group, to remove tree limbs from his yard after a windstorm. At 6'6", Eric was almost as tall as his dad, Stan, but not as muscular. Eric agreed to remove the limbs from Jimmy's yard, haul them off, and dump them. Jimmy gave Eric a certificate that would allow him to dump the limbs for free, Monday through Friday. Eric chose instead to dump the brush on Saturday and had to pay a fee to do so. Eric then called Jimmy at home, from his dad's trucking company, and told Jimmy that he needed to pay him back for the dumping fee.

Jimmy asked, "Why didn't you use the certificate I gave you to dump it for free?"

Eric said, "Fine!" and then hung up on Jimmy.

Jimmy called him back, and Eric's dad answered the phone. "May I speak to Eric, please?" Jimmy asked.

"You've already spoken to Eric," Stan replied. "Now you're going to talk to me."

Stan yelled at Jimmy for 25 minutes and wouldn't let him speak. Stan threatened to have Jimmy fired from the church. He told Jimmy that even though it was a hassle to find a youth pastor, he'd find people to do it if Jimmy didn't pay his son back for the dumping fee. He called Jimmy names. On and on Stan went, as Jimmy sat at his kitchen table and listened. Finally Stan asked, "So are you going to pay?"

Jimmy said, "Look, I'm really curious about why Eric waited a week to dump the limbs and then dumped them on a Saturday."

That's when Stan yelled, "IF YOU AREN'T GOING TO PAY, THEN I'M COMING OVER TO YOUR HOUSE RIGHT NOW AND I'M GOING TO KICK YOUR &#@!"

Click. He hung up.

Shell-shocked, Jimmy sat with the dead phone to his ear staring into space. He was shaking.

Nothing like that had ever happened to him before. This was new territory. Was he going to be fired? Was Stan coming over? Should he get the baseball bat out of the closet for protection? Confusion set in. Jimmy felt lost and uncertain. The ground under his feet seemed shaky. He needed help.

Jimmy called Dan, his even-keeled, steady, straight-laced senior pastor. Dan never raised his voice at anyone. He was a thinker, not a battler. Dan rarely showed emotion—ever. Dan told Jimmy to meet him at the church. (He may have been trying to get Jimmy away from his house.) Jimmy sat in Dan's office and told him the story. Dan listened carefully and asked a few questions for clarity. Then Dan asked Jimmy to step out of the room for a moment while he called Stan.

Jimmy could only hear a bit of the conversation from where he was, but he did hear these statements above the rest because Dan was talking very loudly and very sternly.

"Stan, you will never speak to anyone on this staff or in this church like that again, do you understand me? I know you've been in this church a long time, longer than I have, but if anyone is going to be forced to leave, it will not be Jimmy, it will be you. Do I make myself clear?"

Then it hit Jimmy. He wasn't going to lose his job!

The ground below his feet suddenly became more solid and firm. Order was restored to his universe. Dan had Jimmy's back. Dan stepped in, at significant risk to himself and his career, to stand up for his youth pastor. Dan taught Jimmy a lot that day about character, about justice, and about leadership. Dan led with character and courage, and he earned Jimmy's support and loyalty in a powerful way.

For a senior pastor, it's sometimes hard to do what Dan did that day—to back a staff member in such a dramatic way. Some situations are not so clear-cut. It's sometimes hard to know when to step in and protect your youth pastor's back. Some situations may involve great personal or professional risk to you. But leadership (not to mention justice) demands that you act appropriately.

Having your youth pastor's back may mean standing up to large, threatening truck drivers, or it may mean practicing the simple discipline of not listening to someone who's looking to complain about your youth pastor.

HELPING PEOPLE TO THE RIGHT OFFICE

I learned this lesson the hard way years ago as a youth pastor. I was frustrated with my executive pastor, the man I reported to. Instead of going to the executive pastor with my frustrations, though, I went to Phil, the business administrator. I really respected Phil, who had been the CFO of a very large energy company before receiving a very nice golden parachute when the company was bought out. I entered Phil's office and said, "I need to talk. I'm frustrated with [the executive pastor]." Phil interrupted me and said something that changed my perspective and behavior from that moment on.

He said, "You're in the wrong office."

That's all he said and that's all he needed to say. I was wrong, and I knew it. Phil didn't berate me for gossiping, and he didn't listen to my complaint. He simply told me the truth in a creative way. I left knowing that I needed to talk to my executive pastor. The words, "You're in the wrong office," did that for me.

Your youth pastor needs you to do for her what Phil did for my executive pastor. She needs to know that complaints about her will be directed to her. It may not seem pastoral to say, "You're in the wrong office," to a frustrated parent. But it is. It may cause some discomfort to end a 30-minute appointment after five minutes to let someone know that you don't want to hear any more about a staff member. But it's the right thing to do.

Youth pastors want the opportunity to personally work through any issues people may have with them. They want you to redirect criticism their way before you deal with it as the senior pastor.

If, after a face-to-face conversation with the complainer, the youth pastor can't resolve the situation, she may seek your involvement. In the meantime, though, you need to stay out of it.

If a senior pastor allows someone to complain to him about the youth pastor, the youth pastor will feel undermined—and rightfully so, because it sets a precedent. Most folks who have the opportunity to vent to the senior pastor once will likely go to the senior pastor again each time they have a problem. And the youth pastor is left outside the loop. That kind of exclusion will lead to big problems down the road.

The need for coverage goes both ways, of course. Youth pastors need to have their senior pastors' backs as well. Teamwork involves giving extreme support, at great personal risk, to others. That's what being on a team is all about: You have each other's backs.

DISCUSSION QUESTIONS FOR YOU AND YOUR STAFF

1. This chapter begins with the sentence, "This is a big deal." Is it a big deal to you? Why or why not?

2. Tell a story that illustrates what it means to have another staff person's back?

3. Has there been a time when I did this well? If so, what were the circumstances?

4. Has there been a time when you didn't feel as if I had your back? If so, what could I have done differently?

5. In the future, how can we communicate our need for support in situations that arise? Perhaps there's a word or phrase we can drop that will signal our need for support from each other. What might that word or phrase be?

6. As a staff, do we handle complaints well? Do we tell people they're in the wrong office often enough? Give an example.

Chapter Twenty

UNFUNNY JOKES THE CHURCH KEEPS TELLING

I'm disappointed when my pastor, in the context of a staff meeting or a public forum, chooses to use the youth ministry or me personally as an object of teasing or joking or sarcasm, as if to say, "Well, we can't really take him seriously because he's the youth pastor," or "Well, it's not really that big a deal because it's the youth pastor." In fact, that's the exact opposite of what I hope for from my pastor.

—BRUCE

Everyone knows that a requirement for a senior pastor is being quick-witted, perceptive, and having a large catalogue of jokes. Everyone knows that all your jokes are funny, and that it's those poor, unfunny people in the congregation who don't get the jokes who are the problem. But there's one kind of unfunny joke your church must stop telling.

Jokes about youth ministry or about teenagers aren't funny. This is a touchy subject for me to write about because I need to walk a fine line. On the one side, I don't want to make youth pastors seem childish or overly sensitive. My experience has been that the majority of youth pastors are neither childish nor overly sensitive. On the other side, I don't want to seem patronizing to senior pastors who are otherwise thoughtful, intelligent leaders.

The crux of the issue can be found in this question: Can't youth pastors take a joke?

This isn't a matter of youth pastors having thin skin. You can't have super thin skin and be in youth ministry for long, with junior high kids commenting week in and week out on how big your butt is or how fast your hairline is receding. Sure, some youth pastors have thin skin (just like some senior pastors), but that's not why this is an issue.

Chances are that as a pastor, your joking is one of the ways you bond with your staff. Your intentions are good, and you know that playfulness is a very important characteristic of a healthy staff. That's why it's important for you to recognize why jokes about teenagers or the role of the youth pastor should be off-limits.

The youth pastor recognizes and feels more deeply the impact of the systematic abandonment of teenagers in our culture than most other people do.[8] That fact makes her more attuned to comments—whether serious or playful—that perpetuate that sense of abandonment.

Here's another way to look at it. If you'd feel uncomfortable joking about another of your church's ministries in the same way, you shouldn't say it about your youth ministry.

Try this. *Replace...*

"I'm not sure we can listen to you. You're the youth minister, after all. Ha, ha, ha!"

with...

---

[8] To better understand teens today and their sense of abandonment, read Chap Clark's *Hurt: Inside the World of Today's Teenagers* (Grand Rapids, Mich.: BakerAcademic, 2004).

"I'm not sure we can listen to you. You minister to the homeless, after all. Ha, ha, ha!"

Replace...

"This is coming from the guy who works with the youth ministry! Ha, ha, ha!"

with...

"This is coming from the guy who works with the Hispanic ministry! Ha, ha, ha!"

Replace...

"Let's blame it on the youth group. They're always responsible for stuff being broken in the church. Ha ha ha!"

with...

"Let's blame it on the mentally handicapped group. They're always responsible for stuff being broken in the church. Ha, ha, ha!"

Replace...

"Why does a youth pastor need to have leadership and theology books on her shelves? It's just youth ministry. Ha, ha, ha!"

with...

"Why does the Celebrate Recovery pastor need to have leadership and theology books on her shelves? It's just ministry to recovering sex addicts and druggies. Ha, ha, ha!"

That was hard to write. And I hope it was hard to read. Take that into consideration the next time you want to bond with your youth pastor using these kinds of jokes.

Remember, though, this issue's importance doesn't lie with the feelings of the youth pastor. It lies with the fact that teenagers have been systematically abandoned by adults in our culture. They live their lives isolated from adults. Most young people can't name one adult in their lives they consider to be a friend. An adult who knows what's going on in a particular teenager's life is uncommon. Therefore, making jokes about kids and ministry to them doesn't help. Your youth pastor needs you to speak out against destructive or dismissive comments about teenagers.

As a church leader, it's important that you understand this kind of joking is harmful not only when you do it, but also when someone else in your church does it. If you want to show your youth pastor that you value her as a team member and your church's ministry to youth, then address the culture of inappropriate joking directly. To ignore the problem is to give your permission for it to continue.

Teenagers are looked down on in almost every other community in our country. The church needs to be a place where they're loved and accepted—not stereotyped. Church leaders need to lead the charge against unfair jokes and stereotypes about teenagers, youth workers, and youth ministry.

If you're tempted to write this off as a small issue, please don't. Hear what I am saying on behalf of youth pastors and teenagers across the country. Sarcasm and age-oriented jokes are harmful to young people. They contribute to the overall sense of abandonment teenagers feel. Churches who love kids create a culture resistant to unfunny jokes at their expense.

DISCUSSION QUESTIONS FOR YOU AND YOUR STAFF

1. What part of this chapter resonates with you the most? Why?

2. Is this kind of joking something our staff has been guilty of? Explain.

3. What are practical ways we can work together to help our congregation reduce these kinds of comments?

4. Are some instances of this behavior more harmful than others? Explain.

THE THEOLOGICAL YOUTH PASTOR

The stereotypes of the youth pastor who can't be bothered with theology and the senior pastor who can't be bothered with the reality of modern culture are fading. Over the last several years, I've seen an increase in the number of youth pastors who are deeply engaged with theology through reading and dialogue. I'm not suggesting that they're parsing systematic theology, but they are reflecting on the nature of their beliefs as they relate to youth ministry and your church. More and more youth pastors are seeing the importance of letting theology inform how the local church does ministry. This is an exciting time to be working with youth pastors.

Tempering that newfound emphasis on theology is the fact that youth pastors are still trying to connect with teenagers who live in *today's world*. (By contrast, many churches are built to reach people in a world that no longer exists.) Youth pastors don't need a theology imposed on them; they need theological thinkers to work alongside them as they engage culture.

Many senior pastors can learn from youth pastors about what the world outside the church is really like, and what it's becoming. Many youth pastors can learn from senior pastors a theological framework for their ministries—a genuine awareness of what they're saving people from and what they're calling people to.

Chapter Twenty-One

YOUTH ARE THE WORMS

Our church really values teens! It's one of our core values.

—SENIOR PASTOR

If you hook the kids, you get the parents. A great way to grow a church is by getting kids to show up.

—CHURCH LEADER

Too many churches see teenagers as worms. Does yours? Don't be too quick to answer.

Certainly a growing number of churches have developed mission statements and "core values" that state the high priority they place on teenagers and children—and they should be commended. These churches throw a lot of money into staffing the youth and children's ministries, and youth pastors are generally pleased by this. However, youth pastors are discovering an unsettling dynamic in some of these churches: They're finding that the true ministry targets of the church are adults.

The question is, does your church *really* value youth and children?

DOES YOUR CHURCH REALLY VALUE YOUTH?

Sally has attended the same church for more than 20 years. The church building faces a major road, and the church's new addition looks quite impressive from the street. A few years ago, I happened to drive by the church while Sally was in the car with me. I noticed the new playground the church had placed in front of the building, in plain view from the street. I commented on how uncommon it was for a church to build a new building and then put a playground in front of it. That's when Sally made a very interesting comment. She said, "I think they put the playground in front of the church to attract families. What better way to attract young parents than to show them we do great things for kids?"

Does her comment resonate with you? Having a great children's ministry *does* attract parents. However, there's a significant problem with this line of thinking. Many churches that say they value children and teenagers only value them as a way to get to the people they *really* value, the parents. Please don't misunderstand what I'm saying. There are a lot of churches out there that do value children and teenagers. I'm not asking you to be cynical about the church down the street. What I'm talking about is a church that uses young people for propaganda. Using people in any way is at best rude and impersonal and at worst dehumanizing—and contrary to the gospel of Jesus Christ.

A common phrase I hear among church leaders, especially lay leaders, is, "If you hook the kids, you catch the adults. That's how you grow a church." I hear it too often. Maybe you've heard it, too. Maybe you believe it yourself. Let's follow this line of thinking: The church leaders are the fishers. The youth are the worms. The program is the hook. And the parents are the fish. So if you hook the kids on a great program, eventually the parents will bite.

In this line of thinking, how much do the fishers value the worms? Worms are expendable, but they do have value. (Try to catch a fish without a worm.) The problem is, the worms are valued for the wrong reasons. This is a bigger problem than you might think. Just ask the worms how big the problem is; eventually they are consumed in this scenario.

Churches tend to value adults because they value what adults bring to the table. Adult contributions are concrete. They can be measured by the number of dollars tithed, the number of committees joined, and the number of hours volunteered.

But generally speaking, churches that value adults over young people lack imagination.

Churches that value kids, on the other hand, often ooze imagination. When you value young people unconditionally, you begin to understand that adults need kids in their lives in order to fully understand what it means to be human. Young people have something important to show us about the character and nature of God. You need children and youth to be more fully yourself. You need children and teenagers to become the person God had in mind when he created you.

I'm a thirtysomething married guy with elementary-aged kids. My calendar is full of soccer games, karate, scouts, and school activities. There's a gravitational pull for me to spend most of my time with other married thirtysomethings with kids. This isn't intrinsically a bad thing. There are certain things we're all going through together. This is a significant reason why churches offer life-stage classes and groups. If I attended a church in my area and wanted to connect with people, I'd likely join a "married thirtysomething with kids" small group.

Many churches take the same approach with their youth ministries. Middle school students join a middle school small group and go to middle school events. Some may even go to a middle school worship service. Again, this can be a very good experience for early adolescents. But do you remember what a weird time middle school was? There are different rules when you're in middle school. The average middle school is something of a more civilized *Lord of the Flies* island. Overweight kids get picked on. Mentally challenged kids are teased. Some hallways are avoided because of bullies.

Middle school students have a lot of questions about life. After living through that stage of life, you have a different perspective, don't you? You still have questions—maybe even some of the same questions—but you think about them very differently. The thing is the longer middle school students hang out exclusively with other middle school students, the more warped their worldview becomes. It's not because the kids are bad. It's just that their context and worldview are very limited when they're only exposed to 11- to 14-year-olds.

Such a skewed view can have a dramatic impact on how a middle school student sees God. What does God look like when God is viewed exclusively through the eyes of a middle schooler?

The same principle applies to me. If I only spend time with other married thirtysomethings with kids, then my worldview becomes warped. My understanding of God is affected as well. The fact is that I need middle school students in my life to bring me a more accurate portrait of who God is. And middle school students need me. We need each other. We need diversity in our community, or we miss the fullness of God.

Your church needs young people as valued participants in order to be a faithful church. If you don't value the kids in your midst, you're missing out on God's best. Viewing young people as a means to an end not only harms them, it harms your church. A failure to value young people severely limits your church's expressions of faithfulness to Christ. It's time to value young people unequivocally in the local church. It's time we see them as being as valuable as adults, but with different gifts, strengths, and expressions of faithfulness. Our kids aren't bait.

Of course, most church leaders would never be so callous as to actually say that kids are bait to them. And chances are, it would upset you if someone in your church said such a thing. But the issue here isn't a verbal one; it's a functional one. Many churches believe they value kids—but contradict that belief in the way they function.

"NOW GO GET THOSE KIDS"

Alex was a youth pastor in a suburban church. The following is a reconstruction of a conversation between him and the senior pastor of his church. This is a church with a strong reputation in its city for valuing teenagers.

Senior Pastor: I need you to go get some kids.

Alex: What do you mean? Are there some kids who need a ride home from school?

Senior Pastor: [Laughs] No. No. No one needs a ride. There are some kids who are attending First Church down the street, and I want you to go get them.

Alex: What does that mean? Are you asking us to convince kids to stop going to church somewhere else? Which kids are we talking about?

Senior Pastor: Christy, Jamie, Kirsten, Cory, and Blake are all going to First Church now, and I want you to get them to come back.

Alex: Oh. Those kids all go to school with the kids from First, and Cindy is the youth pastor there. She's really great. They fit better at First Church for the long term than at our church. Why would they need to come to our church if they've found a great church where they feel they belong?

Senior Pastor: [A bit frustrated now] Look. If those kids keep going to that church, then their parents will start going to that church. If their parents start going to that church, then their money will start going to that church. And we're getting ready for a capital fund campaign to build a new building. So I want you to go and get those kids.

Alex: Are you asking us to get kids to come to our church for their parents' money?

Senior Pastor: Yes. And I don't think there's anything wrong with that. It takes money to do world-class ministry.

Alex: I won't get kids from another church, where they fit in, for money.

Senior Pastor: I'm telling you that you need to do it. Now go get those kids.

In reading this transcript, each person has a unique perspective. But only one is showing that he values teenagers. The other may value teenagers, but he values something else more.

SELF-ASSESSMENT

If you're not sure how genuinely your church values young people, here are some questions to ask.

1. Are you comfortable with the statement, "A great way to reach adults in our city is to have a great youth ministry"?

2. Are you comfortable with the statement, "A great way to grow a church is to have a great youth ministry, because if you hook the kids, you've caught the parents"?

3. Do you use your children's ministry or youth ministry as an advertisement to parents and other adults in your city?

4. Ask your children's pastor and your youth pastor the following questions:

    a. Do you ever feel like babysitters? If so, why?

    b. Can you give me some examples of when the church devalued young people in order to placate, reach, or connect with adults?

If, after your self-assessment, you believe your church may have been guilty of using kids to reach adults, here are some steps you can take to rectify the problem.

1. If it's appropriate, go to your children's pastor and your youth pastor and ask forgiveness on behalf of yourself and your church.

2. Get their input on how the church can better value children and teenagers.

3. Enlist their support as the church moves toward genuinely valuing young people in the future.

Church leaders who hope for great youth ministries must work to value students by constantly reflecting on their motivation for ministry. Most church leaders like the idea of a great youth ministry, but it's important that church leaders also actually value the kids involved.

DISCUSSION QUESTIONS FOR YOU AND YOUR STAFF

1. What are ways we show that we value teenagers in our congregation?

2. Do our youth feel valued? Have we asked them recently?

3. Are we satisfied with the way our church values children and teenagers? Are our children's pastor and youth pastor satisfied with the way we value children and teenagers?

4. Have we ever fallen into the pattern of valuing kids for the wrong reasons?

5. Go around the room. What's something you've personally learned from a teenager in the last year?

6. What are ways we as church leaders can demonstrate our value for young people?

7. How will we measure our improvement in this area? To whom will we be accountable?

8. Have we been guilty of using kids to reach adults? Are we willing to take the steps for making amends outlined in the chapter?

Chapter Twenty-Two

THE IMAGINARY VACUUM

Most people define learning too narrowly as mere "problem-solving," so they focus on identifying and correcting errors in the external environment. Solving problems is important. But if learning is to persist, managers and employees must also look inward. They need to reflect critically on their own behaviour, identify the ways they often inadvertently contribute to the organization's problems, and then change how they act.

—CHRIS ARGYRIS

Your youth pastor needs you to know that the decisions you make regarding the rest of church impact the health of the youth ministry. And she wants you to care about that fact.

I was talking with Wayne, a senior pastor, about my company's consulting services. Wayne explained his situation this way: "We can't seem to find just the right people for our youth staff. We've been through four middle school pastors in the past five years and three high school pastors in about that same amount of time. We need to find 'just the right people' to join our 'team.'"

"The Riddle Group can support you by..." I began.

Wayne interrupted me. "Look, I have my thumb on everything that goes on in that church and in that youth ministry," he said. "What are you going to tell me that I don't already know?"

I paused, looked him in the eye, and said, "I'm going to tell you why your church has been through seven youth pastors in five years."

At least, that's what I wanted to say.

Instead, I said, "My guess is that it's not about finding the right person for your church. The issue isn't a staffing problem, because after seven different youth pastors it seems like you've probably had every personality type in leadership already. I'd guess that the reason your staff members are leaving is likely something else present within the church."

We didn't get the job.

The weaknesses of your church as a whole will almost invariably be present in your youth ministry as well. If your church struggles with finding volunteers, lack of follow through, laziness, or consumerism, you'll find those same traits in the youth ministry. Likewise, the strengths that characterize your church will be found in the youth ministry, too. If your church gives sacrificially, then it's likely your youth ministry will give sacrificially, too.

THE IMAGINARY VACUUM

There's an assumption among church leaders (including youth pastors) that the youth ministry exists in a vacuum. Some refer to it as a "silo." They believe the youth ministry is unaffected by what happens in the rest of the church.

Here are two scenarios to illustrate this point:

Scenario 1
A church is plagued by conflict, attacks on leadership, distrust, and a decline in attendance. The church's youth ministry is growing. The kids seem to be sheltered from the storm, a notion that offers some consolation to the struggling adults in the church. They like the idea that their kids are okay.

Scenario 2

A church is growing, but the youth ministry seems to be losing numbers and struggling from week to week. Questions are being raised about how well the youth pastor (or other youth staff) fit into your organization.

The perception in both scenarios is that there's some kind of distance or barrier between the youth ministry and the rest of the church. Let's be clear: That's only a perception. There is no barrier between them. The church and youth ministry affect each other in every decision that's made, every behavior pattern that manifests itself, every structural adjustment that's deemed necessary, and each expectation that's communicated.

Though youth ministry doesn't exist in a vacuum, it may display the healthy and unhealthy characteristics of the church in ways that are different from the way the rest of the church displays them. And that can be somewhat misleading for church leaders.

For instance, in Scenario 1, it appears the youth ministry is fine while the church is in conflict. That assumption is drawn from the fact that the youth ministry is growing while the church is declining. To put it another way the health of the church and youth ministry is measured by attendance. And youth group attendance is up. However, under the surface, hidden from the church leaders, is pain that many of the students carry from the conflict their parents are involved in. Additionally, the students are coping with the pain by herding together and withdrawing from the rest of the church. That search for unity has increased the frequency with which youth group members attend—but the reason for their attendance is unhealthy. The motivation for unity is born from anxiety rather than faithfulness. What's more, as a result of the situation the students are learning some codependent behaviors that may lead them to believe that the church is a place where they tolerate pain for their parents' sake.

In Scenario 2, the church seems to be thriving while the youth ministry struggles. Church leaders assume that it's a leadership problem in the youth ministry. They believe that if they hire the right person to lead the team, they'll have a successful youth ministry in their successful church.

However, *healthy* and *successful* are relative terms. In this real-life scenario, the church is attracting a lot of adults to its worship services and making big promises to accommodate new guests and members. The high school ministry is struggling because the very thing that the adults are excited about seems empty and "passionless" to the students. The church's model to attract adults is actually driving older kids to other churches. As it turns out, the low youth ministry numbers were not a leadership issue, but rather the result of several other church issues.

Your church's youth ministry is influenced by every other major ministry in your church. Church leaders who are unwilling to do the hard work of understanding how decisions impact various areas of ministry are ultimately hurting their organization and teenagers.

DISCUSSION QUESTIONS FOR YOU AND YOUR STAFF

1. Are we making assumptions about the youth ministry's being separate from the church's system?

2. Have we made recent decisions that positively or negatively impacted the youth ministry?

3. Which characteristics of our church do we see in the youth ministry?

4. Are there characteristics of our church that we don't see in the youth ministry? If so, which characteristics? Could those characteristics be expressing themselves in other ways?

5. What are some ways we can improve our understanding of how inextricably connected the church and youth ministry are?

Chapter Twenty-Three

THE COMPARISON GAME

Joe and I were having coffee. Joe is an attorney and an influential leader in the church he's attended for years. The church's attendance on any given Sunday is around 600. The church was looking for a youth pastor.

"What do you hope for your church and how it connects with youth?" I asked.

"We want a strong youth program," he replied.

"What does a 'strong youth program' at your church look like in your mind?" I asked.

"I want a ministry like First Church, Christ Community, or Crossings," he told me.

"You realize those youth ministries are very different from each other," I pressed. "The only common element between them is the fact that they're big, right?"

"Well, I don't know anything about what they actually do in those ministries," Joe admitted, "but I've heard of them. I would like a big youth ministry."

"You've only heard of them because they're big," I pointed out. "Each of those churches has more than 4,000 people on Sundays. How many kids do you think is appropriate for your church?"

"I'd like to see 400 kids at our programs," he said. "That would really be something! Maybe I'm shooting too high. But that would be a strong program, wouldn't it!"

"So how are you going to reach 400 kids?" I asked.

His reply? "I don't know. I'm hoping the person we hire will be able to do that."

A NOTE TO THE YOUTH PASTOR

Stop Overselling Yourself and Your Ministry

There's often a pressure (sometimes self-imposed) to oversell yourself in staff meetings, in parent meetings, and in meetings with the congregation. You hear church members say crazy things like, "A great youth ministry grows a church." And when you look around at other churches in your area, you may feel your ministry needs to provide a similar experience. You may even have people telling you they want a youth program like some other church's youth program. The more options people in your city have for youth ministry, the more their expectations rise for your program.

When you oversell yourself and your ministry, it takes away the possibility for people to be surprised by you. The best you can hope for when you oversell yourself is to actually live up to the expectations you've set for yourself—to be as good as you say you are.

A better strategy is to create room to surprise people by underselling yourself and then exceeding expectations. Before the next retreat, set the expectations lower than you normally would and strive to exceed them. If your group averages 60 kids and you meet with your pastor and say, "I'm hoping to have 100 kids at our next event," he's going to be disappointed when only 85 show up. And it will be your fault for raising the expectations. Eighty-five kids would actually be an amazing result! But not if you set the expectations too high.

DON'T GIVE A FORUM TO PEOPLE WHO PLAY THE COMPARISON GAME

Let us reason together for a moment. In what world could 600 adults reach and disciple 400 teenagers in any kind of meaningful way? That kind of talk is not only naive, it can also be harmful if left unchecked.

It's been my experience that the average size of a healthy church's youth program (emphasis on *healthy*)—one that really cares for kids, meets their needs, and reaches out to the community—is roughly 10 percent of the church's Sunday worship attendance. Of course, every church is different. In many smaller churches, 10 percent is completely unreasonable. In many very large churches (more than 3,500 people), the stat is skewed by other factors. That's why it's an average. Some churches that invest significant volunteer manpower in the youth ministry might be able to nurture up to 35 percent of their attendance.

No one benefits when people in the church play the comparison game. The fact is people in your church aren't informed about what's actually happening in other churches, nor are they committed to the values and environments that produced what they seem to like about other churches. Usually what occurs in this situation is that the person compares a less-than-best aspect of your church with the best aspect of another. To put it another way, he compares what he knows about what doesn't work in your church with a small piece of information (usually out of context) he perceives to be good about another church.

This is a destructive line of thinking because every congregation is unique. Every one. Take any two churches in your city that you think might be the same. Maybe you'd pick two churches from the same part of town, same denomination, same socioeconomic makeup, same attendance, same Sunday school program, same worship style, and same meeting times. You'd still find two very different churches.

Comparing your youth pastor or youth ministry to those of the church down the street is always destructive. Certainly there are things we can learn from other church leaders, but what they tell us must always be contextualized.

The youth pastor and youth ministry team needs you, as senior pastor, to confront people in your congregation who play the comparison game. This isn't an argument for maintaining the status quo. Quite the contrary, it's an argument for being the best your particular church can be without settling for being a knock-off of the church down the street.

DISCUSSION QUESTIONS FOR YOU AND YOUR STAFF

1. What sentence stands out most to you in this chapter? Why?

2. Are all comparisons bad? If not, when are they good?

3. Do we give a voice to people who play the comparison game? If so, give me an example.

4. Is there a church I think of other than our own when it comes to youth ministry?

5. Has there been a time when one of us has been frustrated by the comparison game? Or maybe a time when a comparison felt unfair? If so, tell the story.

6. (To the youth pastor) Have you ever been guilty of overselling the youth ministry? What drives you to do that?

Chapter Twenty-Four

EXPECTATIONS

Expectations can be treacherous obstacles to youth pastors. Like buried landmines, there are hopes for your church's youth ministry that your youth pastor doesn't know about—until he steps on one by making a decision that runs counter to those hopes. This probably happens to you, as a senior pastor, too. Over time you've intuitively adapted and learned to look for those expectations in your ministry. Many youth pastors fail to see important unspoken expectations until it's too late. Often it's because the expectations were never communicated to her. And the youth and ministry suffer as a result. Let's take a look at some of the expectations people in your church may have about your youth ministry and your youth pastor.

EXPECTATIONS FOR THE YOUTH MINISTRY PROGRAM

Ask 20 people in your church why your church has a youth ministry, and you'll probably get 20 different answers. Many expectations are reasonable and dovetail nicely with your stated and unstated intention for youth ministry. However, there are other expectations that can create serious problems for you and your youth ministry.

Fix My Kids

Jordon was in ninth grade when I sat down with his adoptive parents. Jordon would soon be returning home from an extended boot-camp school. His parents and I sat in my office and talked about how to best bring Jordon back into life at home and in the real world. I asked his parents if they'd thought through rules regarding which of Jordon's old friends he could have contact with. I asked how discipline would be given and what kind of structure he would have at home. After a few minutes of this, they stopped me. The mother paused and said, "It shouldn't be this hard! It just seems like it should be easier than this. We shouldn't have to think about all of this. He should just do the right thing."

I started to see some of the problem.

Then she said, "What are you and the church going to do to help him adjust? What kinds of activities are you going to provide to keep him busy and out of trouble? How many days a week can he be here at the church? We don't have time to be with him all the time, and we think the church should be helping him adjust his behavior so that he can obey us better."

On another occasion, I was meeting with Mike and the other elders of a church to talk about youth ministry. I asked the group what they, as elders, hoped to see in their future youth ministry. Mike got emotional. "I hope this ministry will connect with kids and help them make good decisions. I personally don't want to lose another kid."

I zeroed in on the words, *I don't want to lose another kid.* I wondered if Mike had a child close to him die. So I asked, "What do you mean 'lose another kid'? In what way did you lose a kid?"

Mike told me that his 22-year-old daughter was living at home. She'd graduated from beauty school and was trying to get a job with an elite salon. According to Mike, she wasn't using drugs or alcohol or messing around with boys. The reason Mike was emotional was that his daughter wouldn't come to his church anymore. She was asking big questions about God and church and refused to attend.

Mike's expectation was clear: The youth ministry needed to keep the kids of the church in the church after they graduated.

Unfortunately, a youth ministry can't undo 15 years of parenting.

Years ago while flipping through a magazine, I discovered a cartoon. In it, a teenager in handcuffs was being escorted by a police officer to a waiting squad car. Nearby, his mother was distraught. The caption read, "Son! Son! Where did your youth ministry go wrong?!"

Measuring Success

The average church measures the success of its youth ministry according to the following criteria:

1. There are no complaints from parents.
2. The kids are having fun and learning something.
3. Church leaders don't hear anything about the youth ministry. (No news is good news.)
4. The kids keep busy with programs.
5. The youth pastor knows all the kids personally and administrates the ministry flawlessly.
6. You have "big numbers" attending the programs.

People have a lot of unhealthy expectations for the youth ministry program. Often, when the program doesn't meet their individual needs, they transfer their expectations to the youth pastor.

EXPECTATIONS FOR THE YOUTH PASTOR

I wish my senior pastor knew that having bunches of high school activities with lots of high school kids around isn't going to resuscitate an unhealthy or dying church.

—ELISHA

I think we need to fire our youth pastor. She never gets the youth group pictures on the bulletin board fast enough.

—VOLUNTEER YOUTH COORDINATOR

Holly wanted to put a Garth Brooks poster on the youth room wall. When I told her no, her mom called my senior pastor to complain. She expected me to comply with her daughter's wishes. (No offense to Garth—he goes to church a few miles from my house. I have a feeling he wouldn't want a picture of him on the youth room wall, either.)

Sven believed his son should have been chosen for the "A" team in the church basketball league. When he wasn't selected, Sven's family left the church for better church basketball options.

Expectations are everywhere. As a pastor, you've probably found yourself in conversations with expectant parishioners thinking, *Is this person serious?*

Some situations are harder than others when it comes to telling people no. When Holly and her mom throw a fit, it's not hard to say no. Sven's situation might be more difficult because you hate to see someone leave the church because of something silly like his son's not being on the church basketball team. Sometimes people can't get what they want, and your experience probably tells you that "No" is a positive answer for your community as a whole.

Inevitably if someone gets frustrated enough regarding unmet expectations with you or your staff, it progresses to being a problem with the ministry itself. Then, if expectations are still unmet, it becomes personal.

In this section, I want to focus on the expectations your church has for the youth ministry and the youth pastor. Your youth pastor can't manage all of the expectations being put on her shoulders.

All Things to All People

I led a seminar with Mark Oestreicher, the president of Youth Specialties, called "The Expectations That Killed the Youth Worker." In it, Mark wrote something that illustrates the expectations placed on the youth pastor. His presentation was very well received and inspired plenty of laughter. Here are some of the highlights.

Selected items from the youth worker's job description, written by the rookie youth worker:

- Hang out with kids, primarily at Taco Bell and other fine dining establishments. (Of course, the church will pay for this food, since it's a ministry expense.)

- Stay current on various gaming systems (Xbox, PS3, Wii)—all for the benefit of the kingdom of God.

- Build strength and ability in various teen-related activities, such as Airsoft, paintball, go-karting, shopping, and movie-going. (Clearly, ability in these areas will provide relational bridges to teenagers.)

Selected items from the youth worker's job description, written by the veteran youth worker:

- Hang at Starbucks, with or without teenagers. The church sees the undeniable ministry validity of this, and will provide an unlimited Starbucks card.

- Provide a steady stream of input to senior pastor on ways to improve his preaching, leadership, personality, and clothing choices.

- Preach whatever, whenever, but with no real responsibility for leading the church.

Selected items from the youth worker's job description, written by the senior pastor:

- Be in the office at the church from 9 a.m to 5 p.m., a minimum of five days a week, plus two evenings per week. We all know that this is where the real ministry takes place. (It goes without saying that you will "wear your best for God" whenever you're in the house of God.)

- Keep the teenagers in line. They can have fun and all, and things like memorizing the books of the Bible would be wonderful. But mostly, keep them in line. This will likely involve sitting with them in the church service and will certainly involve containing them in the youth room at all other times.

- Other tasks as assigned (occasional janitorial duties, running of errands, etc.).

Selected items from the youth worker's job description, written by a parent:

- Spend time with *my* child, not the Johnson's freaky offspring.

- Fix my child. Make sure she is happy and well adjusted.

- Encourage my child toward a high-paying career so he can experience success and be a nice, positive, patriotic, contributing member of society.

Selected items from the youth worker's job description, written by the board:

- Think of the future, young man (or young woman)! Prepare those kids for futures rich with church attendance, compliance, and financial giving (to the church, of course).

- Stay in your pickin' youth room! Why do you think we gave it to you? (Well, *mostly* to you—there *are* other ministries that need it, too.)

- Raise your %@!# numbers! (We can swear, because we're the board!)

Selected items from the youth worker's job description, written by the custodian and church secretary:

- Do your own work.

- Clean your own dang carpeting.

- Do *not* rearrange the chairs.

Unreasonable Expectations

"First Church has had 15 youth pastors in 15 years" is how I began my presentation. That figure proved to be something of a shock to the church leaders assembled in the room.

"Fifteen? Is it really that many?" came the reply. One person put the number at 12 instead. Then I read the names of the 15 people who had dedicated themselves to leading the youth ministry in the church, but for one reason or another hadn't lasted.

Quite simply, the expectations of the church were unreasonable. The youth workers were inexperienced and needed mentoring that they never received. They had ideas that were too far ahead of their time. They thought they were joining a team but instead found themselves on the staff of a micromanager.

The Riddle Group works with dozens of churches every year. One of the common threads present in every congregation, regardless of the denomination or size, is unrealistic expectations.

When I've posed the question, "What *must* be true about the next youth pastor of this church?" here are some of the responses I've received.

- Growth oriented: "Grow the youth group and the church."
- Able to bring all age levels together, including elderly, adults, and kids.
- Full of ideas.
- Approachable for kids and adults.
- Has the ability to be immature.
- Doesn't do immature things.
- Able to laugh occasionally.
- Funny all the time.
- A gifted musician.
- Able to organize good Bible studies.
- Connected with other churches in the area.
- Able to fix all the church's problems.

- Keeps kids from going to another church.

- Should live in our suburb.

- Can entertain the kids.

- Keeps the kids and parents happy.

- A friend to every kid.

- No more than 10 years older than the youth.

- Needs to be the age of a parent.

- It's not about age.

- Married but no kids.

- Married with young kids.

- Married—and spouse must be involved.

- Married and spouse doesn't have to be involved.

- Single and in college.

- Married with teens would be nice.

- Needs to be a Christian but not afraid of being different—like wearing shorts year-round or having tattoos.

What's a poor youth pastor to do—especially when that list only skims the surface? In your church, there are thousands of expectations for the youth pastor that remain unspoken. He typically discovers those expectations only after he fails to meet them.

Be Best Friends with My Kid

One of the most pervasive expectations a youth pastor faces comes from moms and dads looking for a buddy for their kids. What parent doesn't want her child to be friends with a great youth pastor? It's not an unhealthy desire, but it can become an unhealthy expectation when it shifts to a demand.

Great youth pastors want every kid to feel like they belong to the church and to the youth ministry. Great youth pastors want to engage each kid in a significant relationship with an adult in the church. But it's unrealistic and damaging for parents to expect that relationship to be fulfilled exclusively by the youth pastor.

As a senior pastor, you need to make sure that those expectations are nipped in the bud, for several reasons.

1. You never want your youth pastor to feel obligated to spend extra time with a particular student because of parents who are complaining.

2. It's unfair and unrealistic to measure a youth pastor's job performance according to her ability to be friends with people.

3. Unless your church is extremely small, there are just too many kids for one youth pastor to accommodate. And if he singles out one or two kids for special treatment, he sets himself up for charges of favoritism.

4. Some personalities just don't mesh, no matter now hard you try.

5. Often kids have unrealistic expectations of what a relationship with a youth pastor might look like.

The solution to unhealthy expectations for the youth pastor from the congregation may not be for you, as the senior pastor, to correct. Frankly, most senior pastors aren't good at this kind of thing. However, in these situations, the senior pastor must empower the right people to manage congregational expectations.

There will always be crazy, unrealistic, unholy, and well-intentioned-but-inappropriate expectations for pastors and youth pastors. How your church manages those expectations as they reveal themselves is what matters.

MANAGING EXPECTATIONS

If you've taken your church through the process of discovering and clearly articulating why your church has a youth ministry and what it's hoping to accomplish with it, then you've decided if you want to be Church A or Church B. This groundwork is the foundation for managing expectations for your youth pastor. If you've decided Church A is the trajectory you want to be on, then chances are you haven't changed much in your process, job description, and personal expectations. However, if you're changing your trajectory to Church B (or more toward Church B than you had been before), then it has a substantial impact on what you expect from a youth pastor.

The job description you've used to this point probably won't work any longer. It probably had words like *plan, lead, attend, find, develop, recruit,* and *implement,* which all tend to place the responsibility for the planning, leading, and implementation of the youth program squarely on the shoulders of your staff: Church A. It probably says something about finding, recruiting, and developing volunteers to *assist* the youth pastor in the ministry: Church A.

This is where the rubber meets the road for living out a healthy youth ministry and having a healthy youth pastor. It's one thing to talk about letting the family and congregation take responsibility for the spiritual formation of young people, like they committed to do when the children were dedicated or baptized years earlier. It's quite another to change the bad habit of outsourcing that responsibility to a staff person. The way you, as senior pastor, and the other church leaders define what are appropriate and inappropriate expectations will make or break your youth pastor and your church's health.

The job description for a youth pastor in Church B uses words like *orchestrate, oversee, coach,* and phrases like *assist the congregation.* As I describe in chapter 4, the youth pastor's role is dramatically different in Church B.

There will be resistance to this change in the beginning. It might even feel like a 35-pound raccoon. Your church might need time to buy into it a bit more. People will ask, "What are we paying her to do if she isn't leading a program?" or "Why do we have a youth pastor if she isn't hanging out with my kids?"

Once you feel like you, as the leader of the church, have a solid grasp on what the ministry will look like, it will be time to bring in others and educate them on the Church B trajectory. If you have a youth pastor, she needs to be involved in the conversation as well.

Together select four or five trusted adults who are leaders in the congregation to join you. This team will ultimately be the folks who manage expectations for the youth pastor and the program. Together they will detail what those expectations are, with your leadership.

This group is an important team. Managing expectations wisely is as important as anything else you've done to this point. In fact, without a team to manage expectations, the work you've done to this point will likely fall by the wayside. Even in staff-driven churches, it's still a good idea to have a team of people that manages expectations.

The team members should have the following qualities:

- They are trusted by the senior pastor and youth pastor.

- They trust the senior pastor and youth pastor and want the best for both.

- They are trusted by the congregation as a whole. It helps to have at least one person on the team whose opinion is deeply respected.

- They are leaders who understand the vision for the youth ministry and are devoted to it (meaning they spend their time working for it).

- At least one of them should have a steady, even-keeled personality—someone who won't be overly shaken when conflict occurs and won't become reactionary.

- They are or are becoming key leaders who own the youth ministry and the responsibility for spiritually nurturing students in your community.

As I've said in other places in this book, an advisory board will not work for this role. Taking complaints without being involved is a recipe for misunderstandings and further conflict—a situation that will not ultimately lead to real solutions.

However, a team of people invested in moving the congregation toward Church B will handle expectations very well, because those leaders know what the youth ministry is and why the youth pastor is on staff. They are able to redirect people toward health in a unique and powerful way. This takes the pressure off the senior pastor and youth pastor.

I've built a lot of these teams over the years. It takes a bit of time but has long-lasting results. Often we call this group a Lead Team. Its role in Church B has importance beyond managing expectations. Team members share the power of decision-making and living out of the vision, allowing the youth pastor to use her gifts to the fullest without her weaknesses being apparent to the rest of the church.

DISCUSSION QUESTIONS FOR YOU AND YOUR STAFF

1. Has our church clearly articulated why we have a youth ministry and a youth pastor?

2. How does our church measure a successful youth ministry?

3. What are some expectations we've heard over the last few months related to the youth ministry?

4. How do we determine what is an appropriate expectation and what is not?

5. (To the youth pastor) Are there any expectations being placed on you that you're uncomfortable with?

6. What is the best way for the youth pastor to tell someone that he is not going to meet a particular expectation?

7. Do we feel that Church B is who we want to be? Are there any reservations?

8. Can we think of any individuals who meet the criteria for a team member?

Chapter Twenty-Five

LEADERSHIP IN AN ANXIOUS CHURCH

Something is desperately wrong with most churches today. We have many people who are passionate about God and his work, yet who are unconnected to their own emotions or those around them. The combination is deadly, both for the church and the leader's personal life.

—PETER SCAZZERO, *THE EMOTIONALLY HEALTHY CHURCH*[9]

NEW METAPHORS FOR LEADERSHIP

Leading the church is a difficult job. I'm consistently in awe of how nice some people can be in such a mean-spirited system—one that wounds people who try to change it. Of course, not every church is as anxious as that which I'm describing in this chapter. Yet systemic anxiety is so prevalent that I must include it in this book. Because we live in a chronically anxious culture, anxiety will impact your church and your leaders in tangible ways.

There's a need for clearly defined leaders in the church—leaders who qualify for their roles because of their maturity, behavior, and experience. Old-school leadership models were based on linear, positional leaders who led from the front. In those leadership models, motivating

[9] Peter Scazzero with Warren Bird, *The Emotionally Healthy Church* (Grand Rapids, Mich.: Zondervan, 2003), 21-22.

people is of prime importance. Metaphors for this kind of leader are the Coach, the CEO, the General, or the Motivational Speaker.

Today's church (and world) demands a new kind of leader—one who understands that leadership is less about identifying how things are, and more about the relationships between all things. New leaders must understand the system. The church isn't simply a sum of its individual parts. It is the sum of the parts *and* the relationships or spaces between the parts—and how those parts interact.

In this framework, the leader who is able to find ways to differentiate herself from the system at important moments, while still being connected to the system, will thrive. Metaphors for new leaders in the church are that of the Gardener, the Artist, or the Organizational Architect. While "Gardener" doesn't sound as sexy as "General," there's a need to make the shift. Church leaders who are able to lead learning organizations will thrive. As we reorient our understanding of leadership in the church, we find a need for church leaders to express power through their presence and character rather than through inspiration or coercion. Many churches are not ready for this kind of leadership change. But they need it.

Churches often resist leadership; but more often, churches change the way a leader leads. In an anxious church, the ethos of the church pressures the leader to bow to the will of the system. As a result, the leader can no longer distinguish himself from the situation. It takes a continuous, conscious effort to differentiate yourself from the system. For instance, in an emotionally charged or chronically anxious church,[10] people react when something is viewed as a threat to stability or welfare. A leader who has found a way to emotionally set himself apart from the system can respond to the situation in a healthy way.

Responding is healthy. Reacting is unhealthy. The pressure for a church leader in this climate is to react because reactivity is the norm. In essence, the pressure is for a church leader to behave in the same way as the system. And while it's easy to tell the difference in the pages of this book, it is far more difficult to live as a leader. This reactionary environment is born from the inability of individuals to

---

[10] I'm deeply indebted to Edwin H. Freidman for his groundbreaking work on anxious communities. His book *A Failure of Nerve: Leadership in the Age of the Quick Fix* (Seabury Books, 2007) has been a tremendous resource for me in understanding church environments and health.

remove themselves emotionally from a situation in a healthy way. As a church leader in this situation, you'll likely find yourself *reacting* as well, even if you've rarely done so in the past. This emotional reaction also leads to an inability to listen, dialogue, or change opinions in important ways. Leaders in these churches become increasingly unwilling to challenge the status quo, reluctant to move the congregation toward transformation.

IMPLICATIONS FOR YOUTH MINISTRY

This environment has serious implications for your church's youth ministry. Parents are emotionally charged these days. I'm not simply talking about the mama-bear-and-her-cub syndrome. I'm saying there's a disproportionate number of parents in North America who have a constant simmer of anxiety just below the surface. Parents, youth workers, and kids can all be emotionally reactive. Leading in this environment takes more wisdom and maturity than most young youth pastors possess. It demands your involvement and the involvement of other strong leaders who buy into your church's vision to make it happen. Youth ministry (and ministry in general) demands thoughtful responses and appropriate flexibility with regard to schedules and programming, as well as clarity of direction. Reactivity, rigidity of office hours or programming, and lack of clarity all lead to lack of health and are barriers to the dynamic spiritual nurturing of teenagers.

IMPLICATIONS FOR THE YOUTH PASTOR

As naive as some may be, youth pastors enter the ministry in order to help churches usher in the kingdom of God. They have likely heard of church politics, but they have yet to experience leadership in a chronically anxious environment. They simply have no idea about the strength of the constant pressure to placate and comfort these congregations. Change is difficult in these churches. And since youth ministry needs to change often to be effective, it can cause problems. Changes may take the form of adjustments in programming or expectations of the staff. Change is difficult in an anxious church because health isn't the norm and irrationality and immaturity reign. This is compounded by the fact that most youth workers are unaware of the unique expectations being placed on them.

For these reasons, senior pastors need to educate their youth pastors on what leadership means in these churches. They need to teach them how to differentiate themselves from the dysfunction while staying relationally connected, how to respond rather than react, and how the anxious church works.

Emotionally charged churches may have some of the following characteristics:

- Heightened fear of change.

- The traditions or routines of the past overrule biblical faithfulness in decision-making.

- They label themselves as places of refuge or retreat from life.

- They perceive themselves as a church for people wounded by other churches.

- There are cries for a vision. Frustrated people in the congregation may use phrases like, "Where are we going?"

- Cries for unity arise during disagreement.

- They place a strong emphasis on comfort and stability.

- Leaders in the church stop leading or attending.

- Leaders see the church as being in a rut or resistant to change.

TWISTED VALUES

A lay leader in one emotionally charged church expressed his church's position this way: "We've somehow gotten off that track. We must be about the kingdom of God. So what we need to do is make our church more comfortable for people. We need to seek stability and stop making changes that might upset people and seek out unity."

It's tricky, isn't it? Here's an influential lay leader of a church stating a solid biblical value: "We need to be about the kingdom of

God." What Christian doesn't want that? Where the situation gets confusing—and where church leaders can get into trouble—is how this value is lived out.

This lay leader wants to see the kingdom of God displayed in his church. Yet his plan for doing so is contrary to how the kingdom often operates. The kingdom of God wreaks havoc with comfort and turns the lives of those who follow Christ upside down. Stability is an emotional response to a need only Christ can meet. Self-preservation is not an attribute of the kingdom. Unity—in this sense—isn't biblical, either. This layperson wants church leaders to stop upsetting people who don't like change. A cry for unity in this case is nothing more than sacrificing faithfulness for the least mature members of the church. As a result, in this environment, it becomes increasingly difficult to be a leader. These are nuances young leaders rarely pick up on without the guiding leadership of a mentor.

When a church is emotionally unhealthy, it begins to seek out ways to stop the turbulence. A desire for comfort, stability, and unity is how they describe their needs.

A leader in the congregation may seek to be faithful in bringing about the good news of God as she attempts to lead the church out of its rut. However, she'll be met with powerful resistance from the system. It only takes a few leaders attempting this and failing in an emotionally charged environment for the rest of the leaders to stop stepping up to lead.

As this situation plays out, a growing pessimism becomes the norm within the church. Any new initiative is placed under the microscope. People begin to question the integrity of the church's leaders and accuse them of either not leading or having a hidden agenda. Distrust, alienation, and condemnation run rampant. The church may ultimately fracture, split, or get new leadership, which may temporarily lessen the anxiety for a period of time. This is likely part of the pattern the church has experienced throughout its history. Blame for these problems is placed on the leaders, who likely didn't know what hit them. And the community accepts such behavior as normal. The strongest leaders who are able to differentiate themselves from the system will ultimately leave the church and go to an environment where they can lead. This is true of paid staff and lay people. Over the last decade, many denominations have suffered significant loss of strong leadership to nondenominational churches or more healthy denominations because of this pattern.

Pastors in these churches struggle to find other leaders to join them because the least mature are often the individuals the church would have lead them. The high-capacity leaders pull away from leadership in these churches. Because blame is so pervasive, the culture in these churches has consistently demonstrated to the most competent leaders that they will become targets if they choose to lead.

Changing the way your church does youth ministry in these environments can be tricky business. It requires a great deal of experience and wisdom. A youth pastor who's unaware of the environment may set off unhealthy behavior unintentionally. This creates problems not only for the youth pastor, but also for you as the senior pastor. Youth ministry in these churches must be closely connected to the rest of the church leaders.

THE ROOT OF YOUTH MINISTRY STAFFING

An emotionally charged church looks for quick-fix solutions because it has a low tolerance for discomfort or pain. Because distrust is often the default reaction to leaders who don't communicate clearly or who present information in a different way than the church is used to, it creates ambiguity and uncertainty in the minds of the congregation looking for stability and some solid ground to stand on. This low tolerance for discomfort causes the church to react with a desire for the status quo. Since the church is looking for the fastest possible solution to ease their feelings of suffering, they often don't investigate the consequences of the simple solutions they desire. The church often reduces complex situations to overly simple scenarios. Rushing will do that. This may be the single greatest root cause for the unhealthy pattern in staffing for a youth ministry. A great deal of the resistance you may feel while moving from Church A to Church B will be rooted in the value your congregation places on its comfort and relieving its corporate pain.

HIRING A YOUTH PASTOR IN AN ANXIOUS CHURCH

If you are hiring a youth pastor in a chronically anxious church, please let the candidates know that before you hire them. Take extra time to explain the situation so that they know what they might be getting into. For a new youth pastor, these emotional responses can come as a huge surprise. They have simply never seen this side of ministry. The environment I've described might seem normal or even acceptable to you (which, by the way, would be a big problem), but it is not normal or acceptable to most new youth pastors. The initial shock and subsequent wounding of youth pastors (and pastors) accounts for the tremendous rates of dropouts and forced terminations within the church each year.

DISCUSSION QUESTIONS FOR YOU AND YOUR STAFF

1. On a scale of 1 to 10, with 1 being not anxious at all and 10 being highly anxious, where would you rate the anxiety level in our congregation? Tell a story that supports your rating.

2. Are the people connected with the youth ministry (parents, youth, youth workers) more or less anxious than the rest of the congregation? How does that impact the decisions we're making regarding the youth ministry?

3. Does our church have any of the characteristics of an emotionally charged church listed in this chapter? If so, which ones? Explain.

4. Assess yourself. Are you more of a reactive leader or a responsive leader? Explain.

5. What steps do we need to take in order to lead together as a team in our church community? If you were to develop a plan for handling anxiety in the youth ministry, what would it look like?

6. What kind of youth pastor should we be looking for? What do we need to communicate to a candidate before she comes on board?

Chapter Twenty-Six

THE PART-TIME YOUTH PASTOR

I wish my pastor knew how inadequate I feel. How much I really do feel like I'm at the bottom of the totem pole. How I feel like it's my absolute pleasure for being allowed to serve and how I'm waiting every single moment for someone to say, "She's not good enough to continue serving."

I'm not looking for praise or even confirmation. I don't know what I need, I really don't. I do know that what I do is appreciated. I guess that somewhere deep inside me, I never quite feel totally "accepted."

—PEG

Job Posting
Position: Youth Pastor, Part-Time

Description
Responsible for managing three leadership teams for ages 11-22. Will meet with teams on regular basis to pray and plan activities and events.

Requirements

Must love the Lord God with all your heart. Must be a minimum of 25 years old and married with a degree, from seminary or Bible college in biblical studies, or currently in seminary or Bible college to obtain a degree. Must have at least one year of proven experience as lay person or staff working with youth or must have served as a youth camp counselor or some equal experience for at least one year.

Compensation

$150/week

Some of the greatest potential for youth ministry lies within churches that would consider looking for a volunteer or part-time youth pastor. There's so much potential for health, community, and congregational connection within these churches; however, it's too often squandered because the church isn't willing to do a little groundwork.

These churches often suffer from a paradox. They're willing to hire almost anyone who crosses their paths who's even remotely interested in teenagers. Yet they believe the people they hire for a few dollars a week should be satisfied or even joyful for the opportunity to work with students. To put it another way, there's often desperation to find someone simply willing to lead a youth ministry. Once the church finds that person, though, the tables turn. The church acts as though the person should feel privileged to work for them.

WORKING WITH A PART-TIMER

When you hire a part-time youth pastor, it's important to understand a few things. First, part-time people need clearly articulated expectations as much as full-time people do. Those expectations should reflect the amount of time you're paying your part-timer for. Part-time youth pastors need a modified job description that allows them to accomplish what you ask them to do.

To create a workable job description, you have to ask yourself some questions. For example: What do you expect your youth pastor to do? How many hours each week will it take him to do it? Be realistic.

Once you've articulated your expectations, hold your youth pastor to them so that he can be healthy. The job description at the beginning of the chapter is not healthy. The dirty little secret of ministry is that some churches let people work more than they pay them for. This is okay if the environment is healthy, and it's done in short bursts. However, it's not sustainable as a lifestyle. An important aspect of leading a part-time youth pastor is encouraging him to work the number of hours you're paying him for. It's a sin to take advantage of people who will regularly work more than you pay them for. We often spiritualize it and say it's for God, therefore it must be okay. But that's a lie.

Here's how the situation usually goes down. The church can't afford to hire a full-time youth pastor—which is completely okay, because it's expensive to hire full-time staff. But the church doesn't fill in the gaps with volunteers, either. Instead, it hires a workaholic for beans, burns him out, and then finds another. There's a name for this type of behavior. It's called abuse.

It's okay to not have a youth ministry in your church. It's okay to have a very simple youth ministry in your church, without lots of programs. But if you choose to hire a youth pastor, take care of him.

DISCUSSION QUESTIONS FOR YOU AND YOUR STAFF

1. How many hours does our part-time youth pastor work?

2. What do we expect our part-time youth pastor to do?

3. Are we taking advantage of our part-time youth pastor?

It

How Churches and Leaders Can Get It and Keep It

Craig Groeschel

When Craig Groeschel founded LifeChurch. tv, the congregation met in a borrowed two-car garage, with ratty furnishings and faulty audiovisual equipment. But people were drawn there, sensing a powerful, life-changing force Groeschel calls "It."

What is It, and how can you and your ministry get—and keep—It? Combining in-your-face honesty with off-the-wall humor, this book tells how any believer can obtain It, get It back, and guard It.

One of today's most innovative church leaders, Groeschel provides profile interviews with Mark Driscoll, Perry Noble, Tim Stevens, Mark Batterson, Jud Wilhite, and Dino Rizzo.

This lively book will challenge churches and their leaders to maintain the spiritual balance that results in experiencing It in their lives.

hardcover, printed: 978-0-310-28682-0

Pick up a copy today at your favorite bookstore!

Jesus Wants to Save Christians

A Manifesto for the Church in Exile

Rob Bell and Don Golden

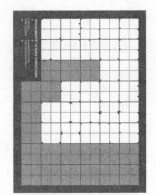

"It's a book about faith and fear,
wealth and war,
poverty, power, safety, terror,
Bibles, bombs, and homeland insecurity.
It's about empty empires and the truth that everybody's a priest, it's about oppression, occupation, and what happens when Christians support, animate and participate in the very things Jesus came to set people free from.

It's about what it means to be a part of the church of Jesus in a world where some people fly planes into buildings while others pick up groceries in Hummers."

hardcover, printed: 978-0-310-27502-2

Pick up a copy today at your favorite bookstore!

ZONDERVAN®
.com

The Monkey and the Fish

Liquid Leadership for a Third-Culture Church

Dave Gibbons

Our world is marked by unprecedented degrees of multiculturalism, ethnic diversity, social shifts, international collaboration, and technology-driven changes. The changes are profound, especially when you consider the unchecked decline in the influence, size, and social standing of the church. There is an undercurrent of anxiety in the evangelical world, and a hunger for something new. And we're sensing the urgency of it.

We need fresh, creative counterintuitive ways of doing ministry and leading the church in the 21st century. We need to adapt. Fast. Both in our practices and our thinking.

The aim of this book is simple: When we understand the powerful forces at work in the world today, we'll learn how something called The Third Culture can yield perhaps the most critical missing ingredient in the church today—adaptability—and help the church remain on the best side of history.

A Third Culture Church and a Third Culture Leader looks at our new global village and the church's role in that village in a revolutionary way. It's a way to reconnect with the historical roots of what Jesus envisioned the church could be—a people known for a brand of love, unity, goodness, and extravagant spirit that defies all conventions. This book is part of the successful Leadership Innovation Series.

softcover: 978-0-310-27602-9

Pick up a copy today at your favorite bookstore!

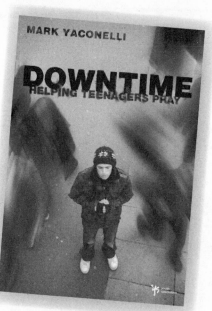

Teens today don't have much downtime in their lives, which is why quiet, reflective time in prayer with God is not usually high on their list of priorities. Here you'll find the tools and insights needed to help teens understand why and how to pray, and to guide them towards a life or prayer.

Downtime
Helping Teenagers Pray
Mark Yaconelli
RETAIL $19.99
ISBN 978-0-310-28362-1

The changes and challenges of adolescence can leave many parents feeling overwhelmed at times with fear, confusion, frustration, and a lack of understanding. But here you'll find hope to help you understand and effectively parent your teen. Dr. Walt Mueller brings more than 30 years of adolescent research (and his own parenting experience) to help you through the tumultuous years of adolescence.

The Space Between
A Parent's Guide to Teenage Development
Walt Mueller
RETAIL $9.99
ISBN 978-0-310-28771-1